Pearson's Car Servicing Series

Mini Clubman and 1275 GT

Including Clubman Estate

D. M. PALMER

D1332747

HAMLYN
London·New York·Sydney·Toronto

Front cover: *Mini Clubman Saloon*   Back cover: *Mini Clubman Estate*

Pearson's Car Servicing Series

Austin A40 Farina

**Austin Cambridge A60 and
Morris Oxford VI**
Also covering Austin A55 Mark II,
Morris Oxford V, M.G. Magnette III, IV,
Riley 4/68, 4/72 and Wolseley 15/60, 16/60.

Ford Anglia 105E
Including 1200 Super Anglia, Estate Cars,
from 1959 and 5/7-cwt Vans from 1961.

Ford Capri

Ford Corsair 1500
Standard and GT Saloons with the
1 498-cm³ in-line engine—models from
October 1963 to September 1965.

Ford Corsair V4
All models from October 1965–1970 with
1 664- and 1 996-cm³ vee-cylinder engines.

Ford Cortina Mark I
Models from 1963–66.

Ford Cortina Mark II
Models from 1967–70.

Ford Escort

**Ford Zephyr 4, 6 and
Zodiac Mark III**
Models produced from April 1962 to April 1966.

Hillman Imp and Singer Chamois
All models, including Sunbeam Sport and
Sunbeam Stiletto.

Hillman Hunter and Minx (from 1967)
Covers the following models:
Hillman Hunter, Minx, Singer Gazelle
and Vogue (from 1967), Sunbeam Rapier
and Humber Sceptre (from 1968),
Sunbeam Alpine and Hillman GT (from 1970).

Hillman Minx Series I–VI
Covering the years 1957–1966, and
including Super Minx models.

Mini and Mini-Cooper
All Morris and Austin Minis from 1959–1969,
and Mini 850, 1000 and Cooper S from 1970.

Mini Clubman and 1275GT

Morris, Austin and M.G. 1100

Morris, Austin and M.G. 1300

**Morris, Austin 1800
and Wolseley 18/85**

Morris Marina

Morris Minor

Triumph Herald

Triumph 1300

**Vauxhall Velox, Cresta, Viscount
and Ventora**

Vauxhall Victor F, FB and FC
All models from February 1957 to
Septemper 1967, including VX 4/90.

Vauxhall Victor FD
All models from October 1967 to
December 1971 with four-cylinder overhead-
camshaft engines, including VX 4/90.

Vauxhall Viva HA

Vauxhall Viva HB
Models from September 1966 to
September 1970.

Vauxhall Viva HC and Firenza

Volkswagen Beetles

Preface

Motor manufacturers all agree that for a car to give its ultimate in performance and reliability it must be regularly and correctly serviced. Almost half the work booked in by the majority of garages takes the form of manufacturer's schedule services and with high labour costs in garages it is little wonder that many owners are carrying out their own servicing.

Whilst this is all very well when the work is carried out properly, some owners with no practical background whatsoever only serve to make their cars less reliable by doing jobs incorrectly. This is no fault of their own. It is due simply to the fact that they have no detailed instructions to follow—and this is where the present series of maintenance books comes to their assistance.

This book covers the Mini Clubman Saloon, Estate and the higher-powered 1275GT introduced October 1969. It is based on the manufacturer's latest servicing schedules, although it is possible that modifications may be introduced to components or schedules from time to time in the light of operating experience. The first few chapters tell the owner what tools and materials he needs, how to road test the vehicle, and sets out in full each service under its appropriate mileage. The subsequent chapters describe how each job contained in the servicing lists is carried out.

Illustrations are clear and precise, the text is easy to understand and contains the minimum of technical terms. It is a book for the untrained owner-driver which enables him to tackle his servicing procedure knowing that he is carrying it out in the correct, professional manner.

Thanks are due to British Leyland (Austin-Morris) Limited for supplying a number of the illustrations. For those equipped to carry out their own major overhauls, a manufacturer's Workshop Manual is available, which can usually be obtained through a British Leyland main dealer.

METRIC CONVERSION FACTORS

To convert	To	Multiply by exactly	Multiply by approx.
inches	millimetres (mm)	25·4	25·40
in²	mm²	645·16	645·16
in³	cubic centimetres (cm³)	16·387 1	16·39
feet	metres (m)	0·304 8	0·30
miles	kilometres (km)	1·609 344	1·61
mile/hr	km/hr	1·609 344	1·61
mile/UK gal	km/litre	0·354 016	0·35
pints	litres*	0·568 245	0·57
UK gal	litres	4·545 96	4·55
oz	grammes (g)	28·349 5	28·35
pounds	kilogrammes (kg)	0·453 592 37	0·45
lb/in²	kg/cm²	0·070 307	0·07
lb-ft (torque)	kg-m	0·138 255	0·14

To convert	To	Multiply by exactly	Multiply by approx.
millimetres (mm)	inches	0·039 370 1	0·04
mm²	in²	0·001 55	0·002
cm³	in³	0·061 023 7	0·06
metres (m)	feet	3·280 84	3·28
kilometres (km)	miles	0·621 371	0·62
km/hr	mile/hr	0·621 371	0·62
km/litre	mile/UK gal	2·824 73	2·82
litres	pints	1·759 8	1·76
litres	UK gal	0·219 976	0·22
grammes (g)	oz	0·035 274	0·035
kilogrammes (kg)	pounds	2·204 62	2·20
kg/cm²	lb/in²	14·223 3	14·22
kg-m (torque)	lb-ft	7·233 01	7·23

miles/UK gal to litres/100 km $= \dfrac{282 \cdot 3}{\text{miles/UK gal}}$

litres/100 km to miles/UK gal $= \dfrac{282 \cdot 3}{\text{litres/100 km}}$

*1 litre = 1 000·028 cm³ (approximately 1 000)

Temperature conversion
Fahrenheit $\frac{9}{5}$ C + 32; Centigrade $\frac{5}{9}$ (F − 32)

Chapter 1

Introduction

After nearly a decade of successful sales and with well over a million satisfied customers around the world, the BMC Mini car range came under close scrutiny by Lord Stokes' team when his Leyland empire took over BMC in 1967. The problem that faced them was how to up-date the Mini without spoiling what had been for eight years a superb design concept, for the last thing they wanted was to be seen as the new owners who ruined a best seller. Their immediate changes, which were seen in the range of cars at the 1967 Motor Show, were mainly to the styling.

During the following two years, a new breed of Mini was developed and reached the market as an addition to the old Mini range. These cars were announced in October 1969, and were designated the Mini Clubman, Clubman Estate and Mini 1275GT.

The models were, of course, immediately under close scrutiny by the motoring press and customers and the consensus of opinion was that the Leyland 'guvnors' had played safe, but at the same time made definite improvements to styling, whilst also carrying out many of the specification changes that customers had been expecting for several years.

In comparison, other than the purely personal decision as to whether the front-end styling was an improvement, the specification changes included: wind-up windows and fully-trimmed door interiors; fresh-air ventilation ducts each side of the facia; concealed door hinges; larger bonnet giving better access to the power unit; restyled and more comfortable seating; facia with the instrument panel in front of the driver; new single-carburetter power unit for the 1275GT.

The cars also contained all of the detail changes that had been incorporated into the Mini range during 1969, the all-synchromesh gearbox, negative earth electrics, small design changes to the engine, transmission and carburation, to mention just a few. However, whilst the rest of the Mini range reverted to the old solid rubber suspension units again, the Clubman and 1275GT were fitted with the liquid-filled Hydrolastic suspension that had proved so successful on the 1100 and 1300 cars. The Clubman Estate, due to its carrying capacity, had to be fitted with solid rubber cone suspension.

Due to continuous criticism, BLMC finally reverted to the tried solid rubber cone suspension, for all models.

MECHANICAL DETAILS

Having dealt with the comparisons, let us now look at these cars as independent models. The Mini Clubman and 1275GT are two-door saloons with all-steel unitary constructed bodies which carry their mechanical components on two strong sub-frames bolted to the front and rear underside of the body. They are front-wheel-drive cars having transversely-mounted power units at the front, containing engine, gearbox and final drive, plus the drive shafts, all in one compact area. The engine itself is a four-cylinder overhead valve (ohv) water-cooled unit with pushrods and rockers, the Clubman engine capacity being 998 cm^3 and the GT 1 275 cm^3. Both engines were developed from the BMC A series design which had so much competition success in the Mini Coopers during the heyday of BMC European Rally involvement.

Directly beneath the engine (in the position normally taken by the sump on conventional cars) is the four-speed all-synchromesh transmission assembly, this being the gearbox and final drive, placed together in a common casing. One lubricating oil looks after the needs of the complete power unit. The final-drive crownwheel assembly is positioned so that it butts out of the rear of the transmission casing to allow the driveshafts to connect up to flanges on each side.

Drive is taken from the engine to the input shaft of the gearbox via 181 mm (7·125 in) diaphragm-spring clutch, hydraulically actuated, through an idler-gear train. The synchromesh assemblies on all forward

1. The Mini 1275GT

gears are of the baulk-ring type. Helical spur gears are used for the final drive, the differential being contained in the crownwheel in the normal way.

Rack-and-pinion steering is situated behind the power unit, which causes the steering column to take a rather upward line into the car body and sets the steering wheel on a flat plane. The Hydrolastic suspension is all-independent, each wheel having its own rubber cone spring unit containing fluid, the front and rear suspension fluid systems on each side being interconnected.

Hydraulic drum brakes are fitted to the Clubman and Estate, with a pressure-limited valve in the system to obviate the risk of the rear brakes locking up under heavy application; the 1275GT has disc brakes at the front and drums at the rear. Pressed-steel wheels have a rim width of 89 mm (3·50 in), and a diameter of 254 mm (10 in)—3·50—10—while the GT wheels are the wider 4½J—10 and are of the special Rostyle type.

The 12-volt negative earth electrical system mainly uses Lucas components, the battery being located in the luggage boot, and an alternator (ac generator) is available as an optional extra in place of the dynamo (dc generator)—although it is standard fitting for export to cold climates.

BODY DETAILS

The body styling is decidedly boxy, as it has to be on a car of this size to offer the most possible passenger space, but the front-end treatment is extremely neat with headlamps recessed in the front grille assembly and the bumper bar set quite high with 'underriders' flanking the front number plate, and side/flasher lamp assemblies set beneath the bumper. The bonnet is almost the full width of the car and continues forward to just lip over the front grille; lifting quite high it offers good access to the power unit. The doors with their concealed hinges open wider than on previous Minis, and this, combined with the new location of the seats, make the cars much easier to get in and out of.

Turning to the interior, the seats are contoured and panelled to offer comfort and support, the upholstery being pvc-coated leather cloth. Floor covering is by carpets, and the area in front of the driver has a protective rubber mat. The front doors are fully trimmed, as are the interiors of the two glove boxes each side of the rear seat. A safety anti-burst door lock, a rear view mirror, and a sun visor are fitted for both the driver and front passenger. Seat-belt mounting points are designed into the unitary constructed body to provide maximum strength and due to the positioning of the power unit there is the greatest possible amount of leg room, much more than one is normally accustomed to in a car of this size.

2. Instruments and controls for Clubman models

For controls not shown, see Fig. 3.
1. Fresh air ventilators
2. Mixture control (choke)
3. Windscreen-wiper switch
4. Ignition/starter switch (now combined with steering-column lock)
5. Lighting switch
6. Speedometer
7. Temperature gauge
8. R.H. direction-indicator warning light (green)
9. Oil-pressure warning light (amber)
10. Windscreen-washer control
11. Heat control
12. Ventilation booster fan switch
13. Air-distribution lever

The bottom-hinged luggage boot lid gives access to a reasonable space, which accommodates the spare wheel (laying flat), the tools, and the battery, leaving room to spare.

Estate cars have an imitation wood trim strip down each side of the body, whilst the 1275GT has its name big and bold in the form of 'sidewinders' along each body sill.

INSTRUMENTS AND CONTROLS

The full width of the car ahead of the driver and passenger is taken up with an open parcel shelf. At the extreme ends of this shelf are situated the fresh-air ventilator controls, that open, close, and swivel to the exact requirements of the operator.

3. Instruments and controls for 1275GT

For other controls, see Fig. 2.
14. L.H. direction-indicator warning light (green)
15. Fuel gauge
16. Main-beam warning light (blue)
17. Tachometer
18. Brake-servo warning light (where fitted)
19. Rear-window demister and warning light
20. Ignition warning light (red)

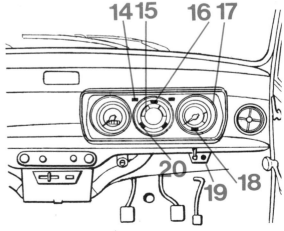

Viewed by the driver through the top of the three-spoke steering wheel is a binnacle containing the main instrumentation; on the left, is an 89 mm (3·50 in) diameter speedometer with mileage indicator, and on the right, a matching circular dial which contains

4. Engine compartment of the Mini Clubman

1. Fusebox
2. Hydrolastic suspension piping
3. Heater inlet hose
4. Brake master-cylinder reservoir
5. Clutch master-cylinder reservoir
6. Throttle cable
7. Air-cleaner wingnut
8. Carburetter damper
9. Fuel line to carburetter
10. Engine breather pipe
11. Windscreen-washer reservoir
12. Heater return hose
13. Windscreen-wiper motor
14. Radiator filler cap
15. Distributor vacuum pipe
16. Radiator top hose
17. Temperature transmitter
18. Dynamo (d.c. generator)
19. Engine oil-filler cap/engine-breather filter
20. Oil-level dipstick
21. Distributor
22. Ignition coil
23. Water control valve for heater
24. Voltage regulator

fuel gauge, water-temperature gauge, and warning lights for oil pressure, ignition, and high beam. On the 1275GT there is a wider binnacle that contains a third instrument—a matching tachometer.

In the centre of the padded lower edge of the parcel shelf is a switch panel which contains the choke control, head and sidelight switch, ignition/starter/column lock, windscreen-wiper switch, and windscreen-washer control. Ranged below this panel are the controls for the fresh-air type heater, which is fitted as standard (see Chapter 6).

Attached to the right-hand side of the steering column, just behind the steering wheel, is a single stalk that operates the direction indicators (up/down movement), the horn (press in), and the headlamp flasher/main beam (pull back towards wheel).

The upright remote-control gear lever is situated just ahead of the gap between the front seats, the gear-change pattern being the usual 'H' formation with 1st and 2nd gears being on the left and reverse being beyond a stop spring over on the right. Where the optional automatic transmission is fitted, the shift lever is in the same place, but operates in a continuous fore/aft line with steps cut into the lever slot to determine the various positions.

GENERAL DATA TABLE

Engine	*Clubman and Estate*	*1275 GT*
Capacity (cm³)	998	1 275
Bore (mm)	64·58	70·64
Stroke (mm)	76·20	81·33
Compression ratio:		
manual transmission	8·3:1	8·0:1
automatic transmission	8·9:1	—
BHP (nett) at rev/min:		
manual	38 at 5 250	59 at 5 300
automatic	41 at 4 850	—
Firing order	1,3,4,2	1, 3, 4, 2
Valve clearance (cold)	0·30 mm (0·012 in)	

Engine lubrication

Sump capacity (incl. filter):	
manual transmission	4·8 litres (8·5 UK pints)
automatic transmission—	
total capacity	7·4 litres (13 UK pints)
refill (approx.)	5 litres (9 UK pints)
Oil pressure:	
running	4·2 kg/cm² (60 lb/in²)
idling	1·05 kg/cm² (15 lb/in²)

Fuel system

Carburetter:		
manual transmission	SU HS2	SU HS4
automatic transmission	SU HS4	—
Needles:		
standard—manual	GX	AC
—automatic	AC	—
rich—manual	M	BQ
—automatic	M1	—
weak—manual	GG	HA
—automatic	HA	—
Tank capacity, litres		
(UK gal)—Saloon	25 (5·5)	25 (5·5)
—Estate	30·4 (6·7)	—

Ignition system

Contact breaker gap	0·38 mm (0·015 in)	
Spark plugs (Champion)	NY9 or N5	NY9
Plug gap	0·64 mm (0·025 in)	
Ignition timing, degrees		
before top dead centre:		
manual transmission	5°	8°
automatic transmission	4°	—

Transmission (manual)

Gearbox ratios—top	1:1	1:1
3rd	1·433:1	1·35:1
2nd	2·218:1	2·07:1
1st	3·525:1	3·30:1
Reverse	3·544:1	3·35:1
Final-drive ratio	3·44:1	3·65:1
from autumn 1971		3·44:1*

Cooling system

Capacity (with heater)	3·56 litres (6·25 UK pints)
Pressure	0·91 kg/cm² (13 lb/in²)
Thermostat opens (choice of three for each car)	74°C (165°F); 82°C (180°F); 88°C (190°F)

Steering

Type	Rack-and-pinion
Turns, lock-to-lock	2·72
Camber angle	1° to 3° positive
Castor angle	3°
Kingpin (swivel-hub) inclination	9°30'
Toe-out	1·6 mm (0·062 in)

Rear suspension

Camber	1° positive
Toe-in	3·18 mm (0·125 in)

Wheels and tyres

Wheel size	3·50—10	4·40J—10
Tyre size	5·20—10	145—10
	(cross-ply)	(radial-ply)
Tyre pressures, kg/cm² (lb/in²):		
front	1·68 (24)	1·96 (28)
rear	1·54 (22)	1·82 (26)

Dimensions

	metres	*(ft in)*
Wheelbase:		
Saloon	2·04	(6 8·16)
Estate	2·14	(7 0)
Overall length:		
Saloon	3·17	(10 4·6)
Estate	3·40	(11 1·9)
Overall width	1·41	(4 7·5)
Overall height	1·35	(4 5·5)
Turning circle:		
Saloon	8·69	(28 6)
Estate	8·84	(29 0)
Ground clearance	156 mm	(6·15 in)

Chapter 2

Road testing for performance

Those owners who like to carry out their own servicing and tuning, need to be able to determine whether their car is performing in the way it should. It is all very well having the knowledge and practice to undertake the type of jobs listed in the maintenance schedules, but unless an owner is able to take the car out for a road test and discover just how 'below par' it is, then it may happen that certain actions are overlooked during a service.

For the purpose of road testing, this chapter quotes several sets of average figures for performance, on both the Clubman and 1275GT models. If an owner finds that his car is not up to these standards, then steps must be taken to restore the lost performance. It must be remembered, however, that the figures given are only a guide and should not be taken as exact; some cars give slightly better performance than others, even when new, so make allowances. The figures should at least provide an approximate expectation of what one should be getting from his car.

There is one further point that must be conveyed; a car cannot be expected to perform properly if the combustion chambers are choked with carbon and the valves in need of grinding. If all tuning and servicing is carried out as recommended, and the car still does not give of its best, then it is very likely that decarbonisation is required. This will become particularly evident the higher the mileage, and even more positive if the engine detonates (pinks) during hard acceleration.

CHOOSING A ROUTE FOR TESTING

Due to the imposition of a 70 mile/hr speed limit on all public roads, the owner will find it virtually impossible to test maximum speed, unless of course he has access to private grounds or manufacturer's test strips. He is therefore advised to concentrate on acceleration tests. If the figures attained are within reasonable limits of those given, then it can be taken as read, that top speed is satisfactory.

All serious road testing requires the use of a stopwatch, and to enable the owner to concentrate solely on his driving, a friend should be employed as an operator. On arriving at the road test location, measure a flat and straight quarter mile stretch, allowing a good run-up and slowing down distance at each end of it. Drive the car over the set distance, using maximum throttle, three times each way, timing each run separately. An accurate top speed can then be calculated using the average time recorded over the total distance travelled.

When taking the acceleration times and speeds through the gears, the watch-operating friend must ride in the car with the driver. These checks can be made over the same course, the stopwatch being started as the clutch is let out and stopped when the speed or maximum revs required is achieved.

Fast gear changing poses the greatest problem when road testing. It is a fact that people's driving abilities differ greatly, so if when testing for acceleration times an owner feels uncertain about racing through the gears, then it is a good idea to allow a friend to drive the car.

When making time checks it is vital that the driving motions are as slick as possible; the car must leave rest in the least possible time and the gears changed on the way through the run with the utmost speed. There is nothing to be ashamed of if somebody else obtains the correct performance figures from your car, when you are unable to; at least it proves there is nothing wrong with the condition of the vehicle, which incidentally, is the sole reason for conducting the tests.

For more normal road testing, where conditions such as engine tick-over speed, overheating tendencies, carburation and fuel consumption are to be checked, pick a route which runs through a fairly busy and built-up area—plenty of stop/starting and gear changes are necessary—then opens out on to a quiet road with fast stretches and one or two hills, to determine the pulling power. Ideally the route should be half town and half country driving and at least ten miles in length.

Over the part of the run in the built-up area, the

points mentioned at the start of the last paragraph can be tested and out of town, acceleration, torque and ignition timing are all put to the test. At the same time, the fuel consumption can be checked over the total duration of the run, and to do this properly, the fuel tank should be filled to the neck of the filler pipe at the very start of the run and a full gallon-can put in the luggage boot. When the run has been completed, top-up the tank using the gallon-can. At the next garage, fill the tank to the same position in the filler neck as before and record the amount of fuel required, from the garage pump meter. Fuel consumption can then be calculated. *Don't forget to refill your can*.

Carry out the driving over the 'mixed' route above in exactly the same way as the car is normally driven, i.e. do not try to drive as if on an economy run. Obviously there is no point in ascertaining the fuel consumption unless the driver puts the car through its regular type of running, so make the fuel consumption run as near as possible a copy of the car's normal useage.

Naturally one must take into account weather conditions when carrying out a road test, as weather conditions and the state of the road surface must play a big part in the resultant performance figures. For example, it is no use taking timed speed tests in a high wind—it only needs a head wind of moderate force to upset the normal performance of the car. Make sure the tests are carried out when there is little or no wind. Similarly it is not possible to take accurate acceleration figures if the road surface is wet; apart from the danger of losing control of the car at speed on the wet surface of the road (which will also have a coating of oil and rubber on it), the front wheels are almost certain to spin under fierce acceleration from rest, a spin which could sustain throughout intermediate gear changes, thus completely invalidating any times that are taken. A fine day will make your test programme more successful.

Above all, if the owner uses a public highway to execute acceleration tests, then he must ensure that no inconvenience or danger is imposed on fellow motorists, or pedestrians.

ROAD TEST DATA

The performance figures quoted in the accompanying table are for cars in the prime of their life, medium mileage, well looked after, regularly serviced, and generally 'feeling good' to the driver. The car should be running on 4 Star fuel (97 minimum octane rating), with one of the manufacturer's recommended oils in the power unit.

The cars used for these figures were completely standard, had covered between 10 000 and 11 000 km (6 000 and 7 000 miles), had all the correct settings for tappets, ignition timing, spark plugs and contact points, and the brakes were properly adjusted.

CONVERSION KITS

There are many manufacturers of engine tuning kits for Minis, both for the standard and the 1275GT models. Most of them advertise their wares regularly in the motoring press and one can find high compression gas-flowed heads; special carburetter kits; exhaust systems; high-lift camshafts etc. However, if these are fitted to a new car, in many cases the BLMC warranty is invalidated, so if a tuning kit is intended to be fitted to a car still under warranty, check with British Leyland first. In fact, British Leyland themselves have a 'Special Tuning Department' at Abingdon that specialises in factory-approved modifications for higher performance. These kits and other parts are marketed through a selection of British Leyland dealers, and if any trouble is encountered obtaining equipment, a letter to British Leyland Motor Corporation, Special Tuning Department, Abingdon, Berks., will bring the required results.

PERFORMANCE DATA

	Clubman and Estate		1275 GT	
Fuel rating 4 Star (97 octane)				
Fuel consumption, litres/100 km (mile/UK gal) At constant speeds in top gear km/h (mile/h)				
48 (30)	4·8	(59)	6·0	(47)
64 (40)	5·5	(51)	7·2	(39)
80 (50)	6·1	(46)	7·4	(38)
96 (60)	7·6	(37)	8·6	(33)
112 (70)	9·7	(29)	10·1	(28)
128 (80)	–	–	11·8	(24)
Overall consumption*	8·3	(34)	9·4	(30)
Maximum speed, km/h (mile/h) Over a straight mile	120	(75)	140	(88)
Best intermediate gear speeds km/h (mile/h):				
third	101	(63)	116	(72)
second	66	(41)	76	(47)
first	42	(26)	48	(30)
Acceleration (seconds) From rest through gears to km/h (mile/h)				
48 (30)	5·8		4·3	
64 (40)	9·7		6·4	
80 (50)	16·0		9·8	
96 (60)	26·0		14·2	
112 (70)	–		21·0	
Standing (¼ mile)	23·6		19·2	
In top gear:				
32–64 (20–40)	13·5		8·5	
48–80 (30–50)	15·8		8·7	
64–96 (40–60)	20·0		10·0	
80–112 (50–70)	–		11·5	

*Taken in all kinds of traffic conditions.

Chapter 3

Routine maintenance

The well-maintained car rewards its owner with the maximum of trouble-free motoring. Many a roadside breakdown is due solely to the indifference of the owner, and would not have occurred if the car had been regularly cared for. Regular lubrication and attention to the items that are indicated in the manufacturer's maintenance schedules will not only help to reduce wear and tear, but will ensure that the car retains its resale value.

MAINTENANCE SCHEDULE
Every week or before a long journey
Check oil level in engine/transmission unit.
Check tyre pressures.
Check level of electrolyte in battery.
Check wheel nuts for tightness.
Check water level in radiator, and top-up if necessary.

Every 5 000 km (3 000 miles)
In addition to the weekly checks, carry out the following operations.
Check water level in windscreen-washer reservoir.
Check fan belt tension and adjust if necessary.
Check level of fluid in clutch reservoir.
Top up carburetter damper oilwell.
Examine steering-rack rubber gaiters for oil leaks.
Inspect steering joints for looseness or wear.
Check level of fluid in brake master-cylinder reservoir.
Adjust brakes and handbrake if necessary.
Make sure that lamps, indicators, horn and windscreen wipers are all working.
Check and adjust headlamp beam setting.
Inspect exhaust system for corrosion or looseness.
Examine tyres for depth of tread, cuts, bulges etc.
Check security and condition of seat belts.

Every 10 000 km (6 000 miles)
In addition to work above for 5 000-km service, carry out the following operations:
Change engine/transmission oil and fit new oil-filter element.

Check and adjust valve-rocker clearances.
Check carburetter mixture and idle settings and adjust if necessary.
Examine cooling and heater systems for leaks.
Lubricate accelerator-pedal fulcrum and cable.
Clean and adjust spark plugs.
Check and adjust distributor contact-breaker points.
Lubricate distributor.
Check ignition timing and adjust if necessary.
Check clearance at clutch-lever return stop.
Check front-wheel alignment.
Lubricate all grease nipples.
Inspect brake pads and discs for wear.
Lubricate dynamo end bush.
Lubricate all door, bonnet and boot locks, and hinges.

Every 20 000 km (12 000 miles)
In addition to work above for 10 000 km service, carry out the following operations:
Fit new paper element to air cleaner.
Fit new oil-filler cap and filter assembly.
Fit new set of spark plugs.
Examine brake linings for wear and clean out brake drums.

It has been advised by the brake manufacturers that at intervals not exceeding 18 months or 40 000 km (24 000 miles), whichever occurs first, the hydraulic fluid in the braking system should be drained off and refilled with new fluid of the recommended type. In addition, at intervals not exceeding three years or about 65 000 km (40 000 miles), new exchange cylinders and brake hoses should be fitted—a recommended job for your local dealer or distributor.

TOOLS REQUIRED
For the carrying out of normal maintenance schedules the tool-kit required by the owner is not too great, and indeed many people will already have many of the tools, while do-it-yourself enthusiasts will probably have them all. However, the following items should be readily available:

Set of 6 open-ended spanners from $\frac{5}{16}$ in to $\frac{7}{8}$ in AF.

A $\frac{15}{16}$ in AF ring spanner for the power-unit drain plug.

Medium screwdriver.

Small screwdriver.

Phillips screwdrivers (small and medium).

Pair of pliers.

Pair of side-cutters.

Squirt oilcan.

Set of feeler gauges.

Set of 6 ring spanners from $\frac{5}{16}$ in to $\frac{7}{8}$ in AF.

Spark plug spanner and tommy bar.

Battery filler.

Tyre pressure gauge.

Grease gun of fairly high pressure.

It may be mentioned that a supplementary tool kit is available from all BLMC distributors (Part No. AKF1596), which consists of a waterproof canvas roll containing:

6 AF spanners from $\frac{5}{16}$ in to $\frac{7}{8}$ in, a pair of 6 in pliers, 7 in $\times$ $\frac{3}{8}$ in tommy bar, one $\frac{1}{2}$ in $\times$ $\frac{9}{16}$ in AF tubular spanner and two screwdrivers.

MAINTENANCE MATERIALS

To carry out the various services, the owner will need to stock in his garage the correct quantities of materials with which to do the different jobs. If the following items are held as stock and replenished immediately after use, there will be no chance of starting a service and suddenly finding for instance, that there is not enough oil or grease.

The choice of oil that is used by the owner is entirely up to him, providing it is one of the recommended lubricants listed in this chapter. The manufacturers of cars are most adamant that only oils approved by them should be used in their units, for these are the only makes of lubricant that have been tested by them satisfactorily. The stock should comprise the following:

A quantity of engine lubricating oil, say 6·8 litres (1·5 UK gal). This can also be used for other jobs such as oiling locks and hinges, as well as being used in the power unit.

A tin of UNIPART 410 or 550 brake fluid for cars with drum brakes. For disc/drum-braked models obtain a tin of UNIPART 550 brake fluid. An alternative fluid for all models is Lockheed 329S Universal Brake Fluid.

Tin of lithium-based grease.

Bottle of distilled water.

RUNNING SPARES

It is the wise owner indeed that keeps a small stock of running spares. There is nothing more frustrating than to commence a service on a Sunday morning and find that you have to fit new plugs, change an

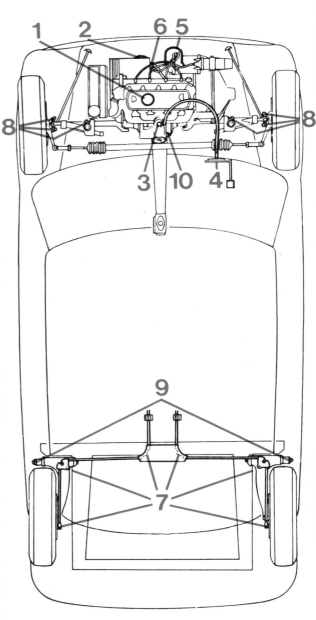

5. Lubrication chart

1. *Engine/transmission filler cap*
2. *Oil-filter element*
3. *Carburetter dashpot*
4. *Accelerator pivot and cable*
5. *Distributor*
6. *Dynamo end bearing*
7. *Handbrake guides and sectors*
8. *Steering/suspension grease nipples*
9. *Rear-suspension grease nipples*
10. *Gear-change shaft grease nipple (attention only required at major overhaul)*

oil filter etc., and not to have the new parts required. It is suggested that the following small stock of spares be kept:

    Set of spark plugs
    Set of contact-breaker points
    Oil-filter element
    Air-cleaner element
    Sidelamp bulbs (two)
    Stop/tail lamp bulbs (two)
    35-amp fuses (two)
    Fan belt
    Rocker-cover gasket

RECOMMENDED LUBRICANTS
The following lubricants are approved by the manufacturers for use on the components given below.

Power unit
Multigrade oils for *all* power units (all temperatures above $-12°C$ ($10°F$): BP Super Visco-Static 20W/50; Castrol XL (20W/50) or GTX; Duckham's Q20-50; Esso Extra Motor Oil 20W/50; Filtrate Super 20W/50; Mobil Special 20W/50; Shell Super Motor Oil 100 20/50; Sternol Super WW Motor Oil.

Conventional oils of single viscosity made by the same companies are also approved if the owner prefers this type of lubricant.

Grease nipples and hubs
Duckhams LB10 grease; Castrolease LM; Esso Multipurpose grease H; Mobilgrease MP; Shell Retinax A; BP Energrease L2; Filtrate Super Lithium grease; Sternol Ambroline LHT.

Steering gear
Use an SAE 90 Extreme Pressure oil.

Carburetter dashpot and oiling points
Use lubricant as listed for power unit, if multigrade. If not, an oil of SAE 20 viscosity.

JACKING UP THE CAR
Before jacking, make sure the car is on level ground and has the handbrake applied when the front wheels are being raised. As an additional safety precaution, chock at least one of the wheels not being raised.

Saloon cars
When using the normal screw-jack as supplied with the car it is very important that the arm of the jack is pushed right home into its socket. If this is not done there is a chance that the threaded portion of the jack will bend when the full weight of the car is felt upon it.

To jack up the car remove the rubber plug from the end of the socket below the door, insert the jacking arm, allowing the jack to lean outwards slightly at

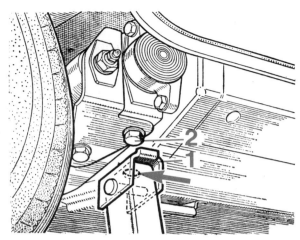

6. Jacking up a rear wheel on the Mini Clubman Estate car
The jack head (1) is located under the rear subframe, directly below the radius-arm mounting. The tongue of the jack head should abut against the outer face of the sub-frame and the hole in the jack head (arrowed) must register over the screw head (2), which projects from the lower face of the sub-frame.

the top, hold the jacking bar (which is also the wheelbrace) on to the nut at the top of the thread and turn in a clockwise direction until that side of the car begins to lift.

Estate cars
The Clubman Estate is equipped with a pyramid-type jack which has a projecting tongue on the jack head. The correct location of the jack, for raising either front wheel, is with the jack head in contact with the sub-frame crossmember (close to the sub-frame sidemember), with the tongue of the jack facing rearwards.

The location of the jack for raising a rear wheel is shown in Fig. 6.

Additional supports
When working on a car supported by a jack, *always* have some kind of support under the frame of the car as well; it is so easy for a car to slip off a jack, especially if the person underneath is pulling or pushing some part and rocking the whole car about. Place the support under front and rear of the car if a whole side is lifted (under each side if front or rear is lifted), then let the jack down slowly until the car is just resting on the support, leaving the jack to take the remaining weight.

Chapter 4

Engine

Both the Clubman and 1275GT engines are basically the same in design, and externally there is very little visible difference, the extra capacity with the GT version being achieved by increasing both the bore and stroke (see Chapter 1 under General data). The engines have a pressed-steel rocker cover, in which the oil-filler cap is situated and beneath which is the cylinder head with the inlet and exhaust manifolds attached to one side and the spark plugs running down the other. The head sits on a cast-iron block which contains the pistons, connecting rods, crankshaft, flywheel etc. Placed beneath the block (in the sump position on conventional engines) is a casing which contains the gearbox and final-drive components.

The engines have four cylinders with overhead valves operated by pushrods, the valves being set in-line on the right-hand side of the cylinder head (when viewed from the driver's seat). Rocker adjustment is by the normal screw and locknut method, the valve stems, springs and rockers being exposed by simply removing the pressed-steel rocker cover. Cylinder-head combustion chambers are bath-tub shaped and the valve stems have oil-seal rings fitted.

Inside the engine compartment, the complete power unit is mounted transversely on flexible rubber mountings and short drive-shafts transmit the power to the front road wheels. Below the cylinder head are located aluminium, solid-skirt, dished-crown pistons, each having two compression and one oil-control rings and running in the cylinders of the cast-iron block. Piston gudgeon pins are a press fit in the steel-forged connecting rods, the big-end bearings being steel-lined reticular tin. The shells in each connecting rod are renewable.

A roller chain drives the camshaft from a spocket on the front of the crankshaft and employs rubber chain tensioners for quiet running. The camshaft runs in three bearings and provides the drive power for the distributor from a helical gear, placed about two thirds of the way down the shaft. Engine lubrication

is by means of an integral rotor-type pump at the rear of the crankcase, which is also driven by the camshaft. The oil is drawn up from the base of the transmission casing and delivered to an external full-flow oil filter, from there, being pumped through drilled galleries to the main, big-end and camshaft bearings. The connecting rods are also drilled so that oil is quickly supplied to the cylinder-bore walls, whilst the rocker gear receives oil at reduced pressure via the front-camshaft bearing. As the oil passes down through the tappet chest on its way back to the transmission case it lubricates the tappet blocks.

Situated in the side of the cylinder block so that it locates with the rear of the main oil gallery is an electric switch that operates the oil-pressure warning light on the facia. This switch cuts out at the minimum allowable oil pressure, thus causing the facia light to come on. The engine has a closed-circuit breathing system for crankcase ventilation; pressure build-up in the crankcase is released through a breather pipe in the tappet side cover—the fumes pass through an oil separator to trap any oil mist—then return to the inlet manifold so that no contaminated air from the engine reaches the atmosphere. Fresh air enters the engine through the combined oil filler cap and filter.

Engine cooling (which is covered in full later) is by the conventional water radiator, located in the left-hand side wing valence, this being a three-row copper-cored unit connected to the engine by hoses at its top and bottom tanks. There is an eleven-bladed plastic fan driven from the crankshaft pulley and the system is pressurised at 0.9 kg/cm^2 (13 lb/in^2) and is thermostatically controlled.

LUBRICATION MAINTENANCE

As the engine, gearbox and final drive are all together in one unit on these cars, it is of vital importance that regular maintenance is carried out. Oil changing and filter changing are most imperative, and if left for long periods, do more damage to moving parts than anything else—abrasive matter enters the oil stream from

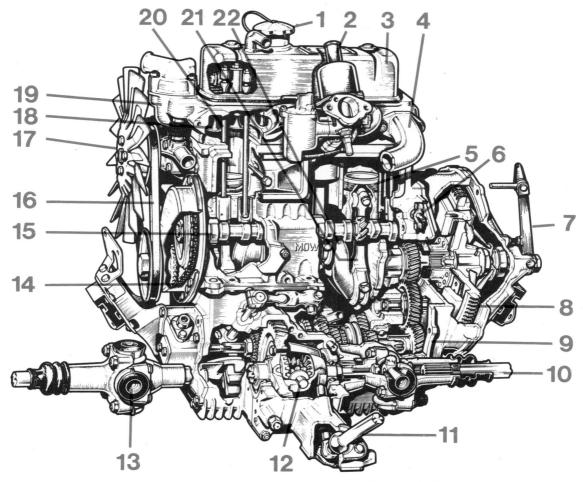

7. The power unit

The gearbox is located under the engine, in the position occupied by the oil sump in a conventional engine.

1. Combined oil filler cap/filter
2. Carburetter
3. Valve-rocker cover
4. Exhaust manifold
5. Piston
6. Drain tap (drain plug on later models)
7. Clutch-operating lever
8. Flywheel starter-ring gear
9. Gearbox casing, cut away to show gears
10. Drive shaft to road wheel
11. Gear-change lever
12. Differential gear
13. Inner universal joint
14. Timing chain
15. Camshaft
16. Fan belt
17. Fan
18. Valve
19. Thermostat housing
20. Push-rod
21. Connecting rod
22. Crankshaft

several different sources and if the filter becomes clogged, it is by-passed, resulting in unfiltered oil scouring its way round the engine bearings, gears and differential.

Naturally the other engine ancillaries need regular attention too, for if the valve rockers, spark plugs or contact points are neglected for long periods, engine performance will soon deteriorate, bringing with it heavy fuel consumption and excessive wear.

The oil-pressure warning light on the facia is the drivers' key to the condition of the engine lubrication system. If it ever comes on permanently whilst the car is being driven along, *stop immediately*, otherwise serious damage may be inflicted on the engine bear-

8. Power-unit oil change
The oil-drain plug is situated at the rear-end right-hand side of the transmission casing. By removing the plug, engine, gearbox and differential are all drained together. Drain the oil when hot and use a receptacle of sufficient capacity to hold all the oil.

ings. This should never come about however, if the recommended maintenance schedule is adhered to.

Oil change

The oil level in the power unit should be checked weekly if the car is used daily and replenished if necessary, with one of the recommended oils. The dipstick is situated to the rear of the dynamo, below the centre two spark plugs; it enters the crankcase via a narrow metal pipe. Dipstick markings indicate Max and Min—these being self explanatory. On automatic transmission models, the oil level is checked after running the engine for two minutes (see under 'Automatic transmission servicing' in Chapter 9).

Every 10 000 km (6 000 miles), the old oil should be drained from the power unit and new oil put in. At the same time, the oil-filter element should be changed. The drain plug is situated on the rear face of the transmission casing, on the right-hand side of the engine.

It is always preferable to drain oil when it is hot, i.e. after a run, because it flows more freely, bringing with it any particles of grit or abrasive matter that may have been held in the oil in suspension. The drain plug has a magnet attached to it that collects any grindings or slivers of metal that may have entered the oil during running; on removing the plug, wipe the magnet clean whilst the oil is draining off, making sure that its washer is in good condition, and then replace the plug tightly.

Pour in the new oil through the filler orifice in the engine rocker cover, allowing time for it to settle in the transmission case before taking a dipstick reading. The capacity of the power unit (engine and trans-

mission) is 4·8 litres (8·5 UK pints); this includes the filter.

On automatic transmission models, the refill capacity is approximately 5 litres (9 UK pints)—total capacity is 7·4 litres (13 UK pints).

Oil pressure

The correct running and idling oil pressures are listed under 'General Data' in Chapter 1, but as these cars are only fitted with a pressure warning light, it is only possible for the owner to discover that the pressure has dropped below its lowest permissable level. If this happens and the light comes on it could be due to any one of the following:

(a) Lack of oil in the power unit—if the oil level in the unit drops below the safe level the pressure warning light will come on. Therefore, check the oil level first.

(b) If the main and big-end bearings to which the oil is fed under pressure are badly worn, the oil will escape more freely from them and a resulting drop in oil pressure will be noticed. If this is the trouble, however, when the engine is running, the bearings will be heard to be knocking, particularly under heavy load.

(c) A choked strainer in the transmission casing could well be the cause of low oil pressure. The power unit has to be taken out and split before this can be attended to—but not until all other possibilities have been ruled out.

9. Location of oil filter and interior of filter bowl—manual gearbox models
1. *Long securing bolt*
2. *Sealing ring in filter head*
3. *Filter element*
4. *Pressure (seating) plate*
5. *Rubber or felt sealing ring*
6. *Steel washer*
7. *Pressure spring*
8. *Rubber seal*

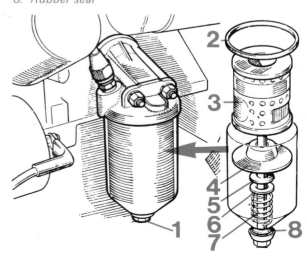

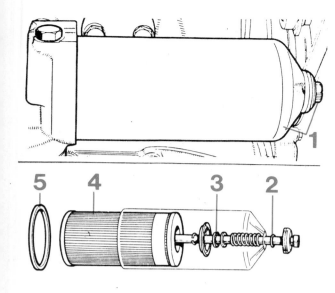

10. Location of oil filter and interior of filter bowl—automatic gearbox models

1. *Main fixing bolts and casing*
2. *Rubber washer*
3. *Rubber sealing ring*
4. *Filter element*
5. *Sealing ring for casing*

(d) Another cause that necessitates the removal of the engine is an air leak on the suction side of the oil pump, but this should first be checked by a British Leyland dealer, who has the equipment, thus avoiding engine removal, unless absolutely necessary.

(e) One final and much rarer point is that continuous cold running and misuse of the choke control will cause oil dilution by the petrol. This will also give rise to a drop in oil pressure, but if the oil is changed at the recommended intervals, the problem will never arise.

Changing an oil-filter element

The oil filter assembly is situated on the side of the engine that faces the front of the car, i.e. behind the front grille panel. A long bolt passes through the filter bowl and element and screws into the filter head, which is attached to the cylinder block. Undo this bolt by lying under the front of the car and using a socket and long extension-bar. When it is completely undone, the filter bowl can be pulled from the rest of the assembly.

Remove the old element and thoroughly wash the bowl in petrol. Renew the rubber ring in the filter head (which the bowl fits against) as this will ensure that there are no oil leaks. Care must be taken to see that the washer below the element inside the bowl is fitted correctly; the small felt or rubber washer must be positioned between the element pressure plate and the metal washer above the spring.

For correct oil filtration it is essential that the felt or rubber washer is in good condition and fits tightly around the securing bolt. A new small rubber seal

should be fitted to the bottom of the bowl and the bolt fully tightened to prevent leaks. This job must be done every 10 000 km (6 000 miles), after the old oil has been drained, but before the new oil is put in.

On automatic transmission models, the oil filter is horizontally mounted.

Combined oil-filler cap and filter

The oil-filler cap, which also incorporates a filter for the closed-circuit crankcase breathing system, should be renewed as a complete unit every 20 000 km (12 000 miles).

Checking for oil leaks

An important point that should always be remembered when trying to trace oil leaks, is that nine times out of ten, the leak is only apparent when the engine is running and the oil is pressurised. Consequently, many people find that their engines use oil heavily, and yet when they check for a leaking gasket they do so when the engine is stationary.

If oil is being lost and a leak is suspected, start the engine and screw the carburetter throttle screw down until a fast tick-over is attained. The obvious points for leaks are where gaskets are used; keeping well away from the fan, look at the following points:

(a) The joint between the rocker cover and the cylinder head—look all the way round the joint to make sure that oil is not trickling down the back of the engine.

(b) The joint between the timing cover and the cylinder block—if there is a leak here it will more than likely be from the bottom of the gasket below the crankshaft pulley, or from the seal in the timing cover around the pulley.

(c) The joint between the engine and the transmission casing (this is where the sump joint is found on normal engine layouts).

(d) The joint between the transmission casing and the differential carrier casing and the oil seals where the drive shafts enter the transmission case.

These are the main points of exit of oil from the unit.

To rectify (a) is quite a simple process; remove the rocker cover (as described later under rocker adjustment) and fit a new cork gasket, tightening the cover down evenly afterwards.

The rectification of (b) is slightly more difficult as the radiator and the fan have to be removed. The large nut securing the crankshaft pulley must be undone and the pulley drawn off its shaft using a special extractor tool, and the timing cover removed by undoing the bolts around its outer edge—fit a new gasket and oil seal before reassembling.

The other two leaks require the removal of the power unit before they can be dealt with, a job best left to a recognised dealer with the proper equipment.

17

TIGHTENING CYLINDER-HEAD AND MANIFOLD NUTS

It is worthwhile, whenever adjusting valve-rocker clearances, to tighten the cylinder-head nuts and manifold nuts. These should not be tightened in a haphazard manner, however, for even spreading of the gaskets, the nuts must be tightened in the order shown in Fig. 11 for the cylinder head, and from the centre outwards for the manifold.

The nuts should be tightened to the torque figure given below and whilst a torque spanner may not be in everyone's tool kit, some garages will lend them out on receipt of a small deposit. The correct torque setting for cylinder-head nuts is 5·5 kg-m (40 lb-ft) and for manifold nuts is 2·1 kg-m (15 lb-ft).

EXHAUST SYSTEM

There are four mounting points for the exhaust system; a clamp where it joins the manifold, a steady bracket between the pipe and the transmission casing, and two brackets between the rear end of the pipe and the rear sub-frame. If ever the clamp at the manifold is disturbed or the exhaust system removed, there is a special routine for realigning the system so that minimum strain is put on it.

To make quite sure that the system is fitted as it should be, always let an official dealer carry out the alignment, for to suffer a fractured exhaust pipe is often very embarrassing and is illegal.

ADJUSTING VALVE-ROCKER CLEARANCES

Every 10 000 km (6 000 miles), the valve-rocker clearances should be checked and adjusted if required. This ensures that the engine gives its best possible performance and that the valves last as long as they should.

Disconnect the rubber pipe (where fitted) between the rocker cover and the air cleaner and remove the cover-securing bolts. Lift off the cover, thus exposing the rocker gear. As there is no starting handle with these vehicles it is advisable to remove the spark plugs before attempting to rotate the engine (see later under 'Rotating the engine').

The valves must be adjusted in the following positions:

Adjust No. 1 with No. 8 fully open
Adjust No. 2 with No. 7 fully open
Adjust No. 3 with No. 6 fully open
Adjust No. 4 with No. 5 fully open
Adjust No. 5 with No. 4 fully open
Adjust No. 6 with No. 3 fully open
Adjust No. 7 with No. 2 fully open
Adjust No. 8 with No. 1 fully open

The clearance for all valves is 0·30 mm (0·012 in) with the engine cold. Slacken the locknut on the adjusting screw of the rocker being worked on, and slide the correct sized feeler gauge into the gap be-

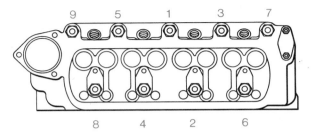

11. Sequence for tightening the cylinder-head nuts

The numbering indicates the sequence in which the cylinder-head nuts should be progressively tightened, in order to avoid distortion of the cylinder head. Where a torque wrench is available, the nuts should be finally tightened to a torque of 5·5 kg-m (40 lb-ft); this will prevent any possibility of overtightening these nuts.

tween the rocker arm and the top of the valve stem. Holding the locknut still, turn the adjusting screw whichever way is necessary to correct the gap. When achieved, hold the screw while the locknut is re-tightened. Finally recheck the gap, and if it is satisfactory rotate the engine until the next valve is in position to be checked.

When refitting the rocker cover always use a new gasket. Make sure it is in contact with the cover all the way around, by tightening the two securing bolts evenly a little at a time, to a torque setting of 0·6 kg-m (4 lb-ft).

12. Valve-clearance adjustment

When adjusting the valve rockers, the clearance should be 0·30 mm (0·012 in) with the engine cold. Adjustment is made at the push-rod end of the rocker. Undo the locknut and turn the adjusting screw.

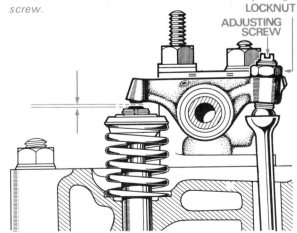

ROTATING THE ENGINE

Rotate the engine by applying a socket to the crankshaft pulley bolt, after selecting neutral.

Two alternative methods of rotating the engine on models fitted with a manual gearbox are: by jacking-up one front wheel, selecting top gear, and rotating the raised wheel or by selecting top gear and physically pushing the car forward. Switch off the ignition before attempting any method of engine rotation.

An alternative method of turning the engine on automatic transmission cars is to insert a screwdriver through the aperture (adjacent to the oil dipstick) on the converter housing and turn the starter ring gear.

DECARBONISING

It is impossible to state a set mileage when the Mini engine should be decarbonised, but generally with overhead-valve engines the need occurs between 50 000 and 65 000 km (30 000 and 40 000 miles), depending upon how the car has been used. If the car has always been driven carefully on the correct fuel, with the correct mixture, the tappets adjusted and plugs and points cleaned and changed at the set periods, then it is possible for an engine to go well beyond the highest mileage stated above.

When the car becomes noticeably sluggish during acceleration, has a higher than normal fuel consumption, and perhaps 'runs-on' after the ignition has been turned off, then the compressions should be tested. If the owner does not possess a compression tester, then any BLMC dealer will take out the spark plugs and run a check on each cylinder's compression.

The cause of compression drop is that the combustion chambers in the cylinder head get heavily coated with carbon deposits. Carbon also builds up on the valve heads, while the valve seats suffer from the high combustion temperatures and no longer provide a perfect seal, thus allowing compression to escape. At the same time, the engine runs hotter due to the carbon so that by the time the ignition is switched off it is glowing red-hot, thus acting as an igniter and giving rise to the running-on.

Having covered the symptoms, let us now look at the remedial action.

Cylinder head removal

Drain off the coolant as described in Chapter 6. Disconnect the battery terminals and release the top hose from the thermostat housing. Remove the air-cleaner assembly from the rear flange of the carburetter and disconnect the distributor vacuum-advance pipe from the carburetter body. Remove the rocker cover, thus exposing the rocker shaft, and evenly slacken the eight nuts (two at the top of each rocker post) that secure the rocker assembly, finally removing them completely.

Lift off the rocker assembly from the cylinder head

and withdraw the eight pushrods, keeping them in their correct order for replacement. Disconnect the breather hose and the fuel feed pipe from the carburetter, then undo the two retaining nuts that secure the carburetter to the inlet manifold flange. Take off the carburetter and lay it at the side of the engine bay so as to obviate the need to disconnect its operating cables.

Disconnect the exhaust pipe from the manifold by undoing the clamp that holds the two necks together and take off the heater hose from the cylinder head. Pull off the snap connector that wires up the temperature gauge to the thermal transmitter situated just beneath the thermostat housing in the cylinder head. Slacken the hose clip around the bottom of the small by-pass hose that is positioned between the water-pump and the underside of the cylinder head. Undo the remaining five cylinder-head nuts that flank the spark plugs and lift the cylinder head evenly upwards until it is clear of the studs. It can then be placed on a bench so that the inlet and exhaust manifolds can be removed.

Cylinder head dismantling

Take out the spark plugs and using a valve-spring compressor remove the split cotters from the stem of each valve in turn. Keep all the valve springs, spring caps, and valves in the correct order so that they are replaced in the same position. Remove the oil-seal rubber rings from each valve stem.

To use the valve-spring compressor correctly, fit the jaws around the first valve-spring cap and place the other end on the valve head in the combustion chamber. Screw the tool down until the valve spring is compressed, whereupon the split cotters can be

13. Removing valve-spring collets while holding spring compressed with special tool

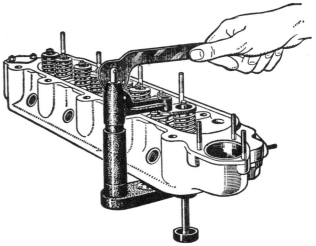

removed from under the groove in the valve stem. Slowly let off the compressor, when the spring can be taken from the top of the cylinder head and the valve withdrawn from the combustion chamber. Then move on to the next valve and repeat the operation, and so on.

Carbon removal

When all the valves have been removed from the cylinder head, the carbon can be cleaned from each of the four combustion chambers. Use a blunt, broad-ended scraper and clean off the carbon, taking care when working near the plug holes not to burr the threads and also when cleaning around the valve ports not to scratch the seats. When all combustion chambers are clean, wash the cylinder head in clean paraffin and dry it, preferably with compressed air, to remove all carbon particles. If the owner has an electric drill with wire brushes, give the combustion chambers and inlet and exhaust ports a final clean with these to provide the cleanest possible surface.

Next, inspect the valves for faults. Clean the carbon from their heads with a wire brush and see if any of the seats are badly burned. If they are, the valve will have to be discarded and a new one purchased in each case. The remaining valves can be refaced on a valve-grinding machine to make sure all pit marks and slight burns are removed, thus meaning a quick trip to the local garage as it is doubtful any owner will have suitable equipment.

Finally wash the valve springs and valves in clean paraffin and lay them out in the correct order again.

Grinding-in valves

With the valves all clean and refaced they must be lapped-in to the cylinder head to ensure a gas-tight seal. Place the first valve in its correct port with the cylinder head supported upside down on the bench so that the valve stem is not touching on anything. This allows the valve head to come into correct contact with its seat in the combustion chamber. Apply some valve-grinding paste to the seat around the valve head and attach a suction-grinding tool to the top of the valve, and let it fall gently onto its seat. Then, using a back-and-forth motion on the grinding tool rub the valve round and round on its seat.

Carry on doing this for several minutes, periodically lifting the valve and putting it down again in a different position on its seat in the combustion chamber. Eventually lift the valve out, wipe away the paste from the valve head and seat, and inspect the results; there should be a smooth, even matt-grey seating showing all the way round the valve head and also around the edge of the port. If any pit marks or scratches are present then continue with the lapping process until they disappear.

After each valve has been lapped-in, wash it

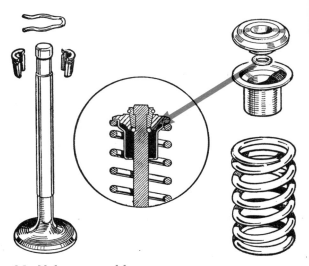

14. Valve assembly
Inset shows how the valve spring is retained and the oil seal located.

thoroughly in petrol to remove all the paste, and repeat for the seat and port in the combustion chamber. Continue this operation until all eight valves have been lapped-in.

Valve replacement

Refit the valves to the cylinder head using the spring

15. Grinding-in a valve using a rubber suction tool (British Leyland tool 18G29)
Roll the tool back and forth so that the valve head is moved with a semi-rotary action on the seat in the head. Occasionally, lift the valve and reposition it in a different position to spread the grinding paste evenly over the seat and valve face.

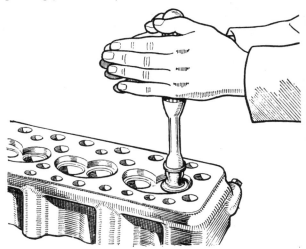

compressor, remembering to add a few drops of oil to each valve stem before fitting it into the guide. With the valve spring compressed by the tool, dip the new rubber ring in thin oil and slip it over the end of the valve stem, positioning it just below the groove for the cotters. Fit the cotters in place and slowly let off the spring until the compressor is free, then inspect the valve stem to see that the cotters are correctly in place before moving onto the next valve.

Cleaning the piston crowns

With the cylinder head assembled, return to the engine in the car and plug all the oil and water holes in the cylinder block with pieces of rag. The piston crowns can now be decarbonised; leave a ring of carbon around the outer circumference of each piston, as this will act as a seal against oil coming up past the rings, but clean the rest of the piston crown of all carbon, taking care not to gouge or score the aluminium pistons.

By rotating the engine (see earlier under 'Rotating the engine'), two pistons will come up to the tops of their bores at a time, these can be cleaned, then the other two can be brought up to the top in the same way. With the pistons cleaned, thoroughly wash the cylinder block with petrol, making sure that there are no carbon particles left in the cylinders themselves, then remove the pieces of rag from the oil and water passages.

Cylinder head replacement

With the head on the bench, fit new gaskets and replace the inlet and exhaust manifolds, tightening their nuts to 2·1 kg-m (15 lb-ft) if a torque wrench is available. Fit the new cylinder-head gasket over the studs on the engine and with a squirt oilcan give each cylinder wall a liberal dose of engine oil all the way round the surface that each piston slides up and down on. Lift the cylinder head and drop it gently and squarely over the studs until it is back in place on the engine.

Fit the five external cylinder-head nuts first and screw them down finger-tight; return the pushrods to their original places and slip the rocker assembly over its studs, locating each pushrod under its rocker before replacing the eight securing nuts, finger-tight. Tighten the cylinder-head nuts in the sequence shown in Fig. 11 to ensure even spreading of the gasket, their final correct torque figure being 5·5 kg-m (40 lb-ft). The four nuts that are solely responsible for the rocker assembly should be tightened to 3·5 kg-m (25 lb-ft).

Refit all the parts to the engine in a reverse procedure to their removal, outlined earlier, using new gaskets where applicable, and not forgetting to re-attach the wire to the temperature gauge thermal transmitter. Replace the spark plugs after cleaning and gapping them, or alternatively, fit a new set. Before refitting the rocker cover, set the valve-rocker clearances as described earlier in this chapter.

Finally replace the cooling-system drain plug and refill the system with the correct mixture of water and anti-freeze as described in Chapter 6.

ENGINE FAULTS AND REMEDIES

The engine faults given below are those which are most commonly encountered and which can be remedied by the owner-driver without having recourse to a garage. It is pointed out that some of the faults such as overheating and loss of power due to incorrect ignition, are not, strictly speaking, engine faults but are nevertheless listed here.

Excessive oil consumption

There are two main reasons for this complaint, the first is faulty oil-seals on the valve stems allowing oil to run down and be burned in the combustion chambers, the second, excessively worn piston rings and cylinder bores which allow oil to come up the bores and be burned that way.

The remedy for the first is to remove the cylinder head, dismantle the valves, fit new seals, and re-assemble. Of course, this should always be done whenever the engine is decarbonised for safety's sake.

In the case of the second, the rectification is more involved. The power unit has to be removed and split from the transmission so that new piston rings and/or a rebore can be carried out, depending upon the extent of the wear.

Lack of power and performance

There are so many different causes for this complaint that the easiest thing to do is list them so that they can be checked through one by one. In many cases, the repairs can be carried out by the owner and full descriptions are given in the respective chapters later in the book, as they are part of normal servicing. Those jobs where instructions are not given are best left to an authorised dealer.

(a) *An air leak into the intake system*—To remedy this, new manifold and carburetter flange gaskets are required; do not use gasket cement on any of these gaskets in an effort to stop an air leak.

(b) *Starvation of carburetter or choked jet*—If the fault is the fuel pump operating at too low a pressure a reconditioned pump is the only answer. Should the carburetter needle and seat or jet be at fault, refer to Chapter 5.

(c) *Mixture strength too weak*—To correct this see Chapter 5.

(d) *Valve-rocker clearances set incorrectly*—Reset the gaps as detailed earlier in this chapter.

(e) *Incorrect valve timing*—This is beyond the scope

of the owner as it invariably stems from worn timing chain and sprockets jumping a link. Dealers have equipment which can check this without dismantling and it is best to let them diagnose for you.

(f) Burned or badly-seated valves—The cylinder head must be taken off and decarbonised, replacing the badly burned valves and reseating and grinding-in the others.

(g) Excess deposits of carbon in the combustion chamber—The same remedy as given above applies—decarbonisation.

(h) Loose leads, or cracked insulation on the leads to the spark plugs—Check and replace as detailed in Chapter 7.

(j) Incorrect ignition timing—To reset the timing, follow the instructions in Chapter 7.

(k) Excessive wear on pistons or bores—This means either new pistons and rings or a rebore depending upon how much wear there is on the cylinders.

(l) Spark plugs dirty or their gaps too wide—See Chapter 7.

(m) Contact-breaker points dirty or their gaps too wide—See Chapter 7.

(n) Leads or low-tension wires to distributor loose.

(p) Capacitor (condenser) in the distributor faulty—A fixing screw for the capacitor also serves as its earth connection.

(q) Battery and/or dynamo faulty—Carry out the checks listed in Chapter 13. If these fail a dealer must be allowed to make further checks with special equipment.

(r) Brakes over-adjusted or handbrake hanging on—Readjust both foot and handbrake circuits as described in Chapter 8.

Overheating

Basically, overheating is a cooling system complaint and therefore the causes of it are given in Chapter 6. It must be remembered that some of the points listed above for lack of power and performance will also cause overheating, therefore, if the cooling system is checked to no avail, then check points (a), (c), (d), (f), (g) and (j) above as they may be the answer.

Engine noises

One of the most difficult things for any engineer to do is to try and diagnose an engine noise from the customer's description, without having the car for examination and testing. Noises can be put into three basic categories; tap, knocks, rattles, as follows:

Taps—When a tapping noise can be distinctly heard at various engine speeds the first thing to check is always the rocker clearances. Should these be properly set, then inspect the distributor mechanical advance/retard mechanism and the distributor drive-shaft for wear. If this is also in order the noise could be coming from worn small ends on the connecting rods or worn tappets in the valve chest.

Knocks—A deeper knocking noise can be caused by big-end or main-bearing shells breaking-up, while a light knock can be worn pistons and bores. The camshaft bearings becoming worn can also emit a knocking noise. Most of these symptoms are accompanied by low oil pressure, so if they are thought to be the trouble have a pressure check made by a dealer.

Rattles—Should the rattling noise come from the front of the engine a slack timing chain is the obvious suspect. If it is from the rear of the engine, the idler-gear bearings and shaft could be worn, or the teeth on the gears themselves worn. Vibrations are also rattles and these can be caused by metal cables touching on the engine; or the exhaust system front mounting being broken away.

It is impossible to be more precise with engine noises than this, as different people hear different noises in different ways. If you are in any doubt as to the cause of a noise and you have checked all the above, then let a dealer test the car, or listen to it and give a report. Professional fitters hear them day in and day out and they naturally get to know one noise from another, by its tone or its intensity, and can give a more-often-than-not accurate diagnosis.

Chapter 5

Fuel system

The basic parts of the fuel system are similar for both Clubman and the 1275GT models. There is a petrol tank, a fuel delivery pump, a carburetter and suitable piping to connect them all. The petrol tank is situated in the luggage boot (upright on the left-hand side) of Saloon models, and under the rear floor of Estate cars. Incorporated in the petrol tank is the fuel-gauge operating unit.

An SU mechanical fuel pump, type AUF 705, is fitted to all models, and is located just beneath the manifolds, such that its operating arm can pass through the crankcase wall and touch on the camshaft. Flexible pipes take the fuel in and out of the pump, the lower of the two pipe connections being the inlet.

An SU HS2 carburetter ($1\frac{1}{4}$-in diameter throttle) is fitted to the manual-transmission Clubman models, while on the Clubman automatic and the 1275GT an HS4 instrument (with $1\frac{1}{2}$-in diameter throttle) is used. The jet size on both carburetters is 2·29 mm (0·090 in). The various sized needles for standard, rich or weak running are given in the General Data Table in Chapter 1.

The air cleaner is of the renewable-element type and is attached to the rear flange of the carburetter. Its casing is quite flat with a top lid that removes, to allow a new paper element to be easily installed.

Fuel rating

All manual-transmission Clubman and 1275GT models should operate satisfactorily on mixture-grade fuel; that is, 3-star petrol of minimum octane rating 94. If a particular brand of petrol causes knocking or pinking (pronounced when pulling hard at low speed with wide throttle opening), either try another manufacturer's 3-star brand or change to a 4-star rating (premium) fuel. On automatic-transmission models, which have higher compression-ratio engines, use 4-star fuel of 97 minimum octane rating. The use of higher octane fuels than these offers no real advantage so far as either performance or fuel economy is concerned.

CHECKING FOR FUEL LEAKS

It is very rare to find leaks in such a simple system, but below are listed the points to check should petrol begin to disappear rapidly:

(a) Carburetter bowl—The most common point of exit for fuel is around the top of the carburetter bowl due to a sticking needle valve which controls the entry of petrol into the float chamber. The remedy for this is covered later under the heading Carburetter.

(b) Flexible pipe between the carburetter and the fuel pump—If there is a leak here it can easily be spotted as the fuel will show up on the pipe and can be seen trickling down. A new pipe may be required, but try tightening the connections first.

(c) Flexible pipe leaving the fuel pump—The same ways of checking and rectifications as in (b) will suffice. A leak from this point will also create a strong odour of petrol inside the vehicle.

(d) Drain plug in the bottom of the fuel tank—If this is leaking, the luggage boot will reek of fuel and will be detectable on the floor, under the tank. The only remedy is to renew the plug, or, if it is the union into which the plug screws that is at fault, the tank will have to be removed and the union soldered. This is a job for the garage, owing to the risk of explosion.

(e) Pipes between fuel pump and carburetter, and tank and fuel pump—These are metal pipes, and if they leak it is probably because they are porous or have been rubbing against something and have been 'holed'. New pipes are the only remedy.

When checking for fuel faults in the carburetter, concentrate on checks (a), (b) and (c). Faults (d) and (e) seldom occur.

SU MECHANICAL FUEL PUMP

Towards the end of 1969, when the Mini range switched to negative-earth electrics, one of the specification changes made was the dropping of the SU electric fuel pump in favour of the new mechanical pump, designated AUF 705. When the Clubman and 1275GT were announced they had the mechanical pump from the outset.

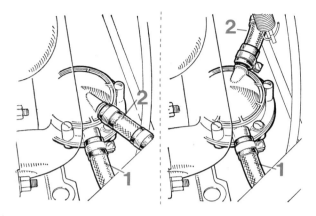

16. Location of SU mechanical fuel pump on rear left-hand side of crankcase beneath exhaust manifold
(left) Clubman cars
(right) 1275GT cars
1. Fuel-inlet pipe
2. Fuel-outlet pipe

The pump is situated on the 'back facing' side of the engine under the manifolds. It has a rocker-type lever passing into the engine and bearing against a cam on the engine camshaft. The pump body itself is in two halves with a flexible diaphragm fitted between them; the top half (which is fitted with a fuel filter) has a detachable top cover for ease of maintenance.

Fuel is drawn into the pump by the diaphragm flexing downwards, thus creating a vacuum in the pump interior; as the operating lever moves off the cam the diaphragm flexes up again forced by a strong return spring, thus pressurising the fuel out of the pump via a one-way valve and cleaning filter and along the delivery pipe to the carburetter bowl.

Servicing the pump
There is no regular maintenance work to be carried out on the pump, but should fuel starvation be traced to this unit at any time it is either possible for the owner to make minor repairs, or alternatively, to fit a complete replacement unit.

To gain access to the pump whilst it is still attached to the engine, one has to reach down under the carburetter to a position low on the cylinder block where the pump is attached. However, it may be found easier to detach the pump from the engine completely to work on it. To do this, simply disconnect the inlet and outlet pipes from the pump body and undo the two nuts that secure the pump flange to the studs on the cylinder block. Tilt the pump slightly as it is withdrawn, to allow the lever to pass through the aperture in the cylinder block and

the pump can then be lifted up from behind the engine and placed on the bench.

In order to check the operating pressure of the pump a special vacuum/pressure gauge is required; if the pump is not working, invariably it is due to a fault in the diaphragm, or blockage of the one-way valve. If pressure testing can be carried out, on the suction (inlet) side of the pump a maximum vacuum of 152 mm (6 in) Hg should be achieved after three full strokes of the pump operating lever; on the delivery (outlet) side of the pump a minimum pressure of 0.21 kg/cm^2 (3 lb/in^2) should be achieved after two full strokes of the operating lever.

A less positive check on the pump can be made by pressing a finger tight over the inlet nozzle of the pump and working the operating lever three times; when taking the finger away from the nozzle a noise due to the vacuum being destroyed should be quite audible. Similarly with the outlet nozzle, after covering it with a finger and working the operating lever just once, it should be possible to feel the pressure behind the finger for at least 15 seconds after the lever has been released.

If the pump has been removed merely for cleaning, then access to the filter is gained by taking out the three screws that secure the pump top cover, and lifting it off. The sealing ring and filter can then be taken out and the filter blown clean with compressed air. To split the pump body into its two halves, the remaining three screws around the circumference of the main pump body also have to be removed. This will allow a new diaphragm to be fitted, but before splitting the pump body be sure to mark the two halves so that they are reassembled in eactly the same position.

To fit replacement spare parts to the pump is often a false economy and in the majority of pump failure cases, it is far better to simply take the old pump to a British Leyland dealer and obtain a factory replacement unit. This will have had all of the worn parts renewed, including the important one-way valve, and the old pump will be taken in part-exchange.

CARBURETTER
The SU constant-vacuum carburetter only contains one jet. Fuel is drawn from the jet by the passage of air at high velocity through the venturi, or choke, the diameter of which is variable. The amount of petrol issuing from the jet is metered by a tapered needle that fits inside the jet and moves up and down in response to different engine speeds and throttle openings, thereby varying the size of the jet orifice.

The choke diameter varies by means of a piston that works in a vertical plane inside a cylinder called a dashpot. The bottom of the piston blanks off the venturi when it is at the bottom of its stroke, and opens it when at the top of its stroke. The carburetter

17. Exploded view of SU mechanical fuel pump

1. *Fuel-outlet cover*
2. *Cover-retaining screws*
3. *Sealing ring*
4. *Filter*
5. *Body-securing screws*
6. *Upper body*
7. *Combined inlet/outlet valve*
8. *Diaphragm/stirrup assembly*
9. *Diaphragm spring*
10. *Crankcase-seal cap*
11. *Crankcase seal*
12. *Lower body*
13. *Rocker-lever tension spring*
14. *Rocker lever*
15. *Rocker-lever pivot pin*
16. *Insulating-block assembly*

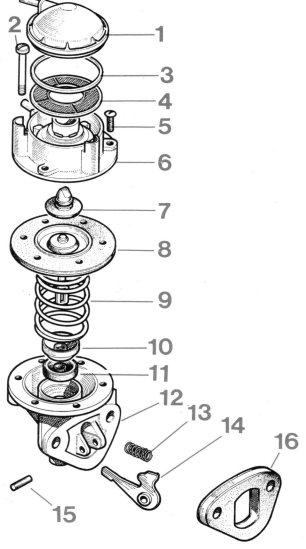

needle is fitted to the underside of the piston and the layout of the various components can be seen in Fig. 18.

A drilling connects the top side of the piston with the engine side of the throttle butterfly, so that the vacuum from the manifold is felt above the piston and draws it up the dashpot. This in turn lifts the needle farther out of the jet and makes the jet orifice larger, allowing more petrol to escape and mix with the volume of air passing through the choke.

Routine maintenance

At 5 000 km (3 000 miles) intervals, the carburetter dashpot oilwell must be topped up with engine oil. This is a most important operation as the piston damper stops fluctuation of the piston inside the dashpot and if the oil level gets low, the damper does not work efficiently, giving rise to bad running.

Unscrew the cap from the dashpot and withdraw it, together with the damper to which it is attached. Using a squirt oilcan, fill the oilwell to approximately 13 mm (0·50 in) above the top of the hollow piston rod and replace the damper and cap. At the same time apply a few drops of oil to the adjusting screws, cables and pivots around the carburetter body.

Cleaning carburetter dashpot and piston

It is recommended that the carburetter dashpot and piston be removed for cleaning every 20 000 km (12 000 miles). Take out the two screws at the base of the dashpot and carefully lift it off the main body; this leaves the piston exposed; lift this straight off the carburetter without tilting, as the needle has to be drawn out of the jet. Remove the dashpot cap and damper and clean the inside of the dashpot with a clean rag moistened in petrol, removing all signs of deposit from the walls. Wipe around the outside of the piston in a similar way, add a few drops of oil to the piston rod *only* and slide the piston back into the dashpot, remembering to fit the spring over the piston rod first.

Fit the piston needle into the jet and turn the piston so that its shank fits over the locating peg, allowing the assembly to drop down on to the carburetter body. The dashpot fits over the piston and can be pushed down on to the main body before the two securing screws are tightened. Finally, top up the piston rod with thin oil and replace the damper and cap.

Cleaning carburetter float chamber

Although it is not on the service schedule some owners may wish to clean out the carburetter bowl during the 20 000 km (12 000 mile) service, or perhaps at some later date. The easiest way to accomplish this is to remove the carburetter completely from the engine. Remove the air cleaner by undoing the securing bolts (described later under Air cleaner) and disconnect the choke and throttle cables from the carburetter. Disconnect the flexible feed pipe from the carburetter bowl and the vacuum pipe that runs to the distributor.

18. Sectional view of the SU HS2 carburetter
1. *Piston-damper oil well*
2. *Piston lifting pin*
3. *Jet-locking nut*
4. *Jet-adjusting nut*
5. *Jet head*
6. *Nylon fuel-feed pipe from float chamber*
7. *Jet needle*
8. *Throttle*
9. *Hole in piston, allowing vacuum existing in this area to be present in the suction chamber above the piston*

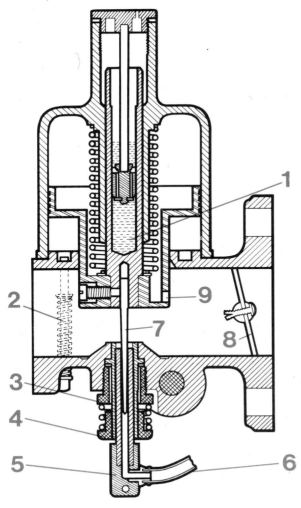

Remove the two bolts holding the carburetter to the inlet manifold and lift off the unit, placing it on the bench. A long bolt (see Fig. 22) passes through the main body from the left-hand side and screws into the float chamber; remove this and disconnect the nylon pipe from the bottom of the bowl, whereupon the bowl will come away from the rest of the carburetter. Remove the three screws securing the bowl cover and lift it off, together with the nylon float which is attached to it by means of a pivot pin; take care not to damage the gasket. Thoroughly clean the bowl of any sediment and then reassemble the parts.

Adjusting the carburetter
The servicing procedure described above should not alter the tune of the carburetter, but it is possible that the jet adjuster may get disturbed, or perhaps as parts begin to wear the carburetter will need retuning. This is not too difficult a job and most owners should be able to do it after a little practice.

Start the engine and run it at a fast idle speed until normal running temperature is reached, then set the throttle-stop adjusting screw so that the engine ticks over at a steady speed. See Fig. 23 (a).

Screw the jet-adjusting nut down, see Fig. 23 (b), thus enriching the mixture, until black, sooty smoke issues from the exhaust pipe and the engine begins to rock badly on its mountings, which shows that the mixture is too rich. Now screw the jet nut into the body again until the engine runs smoothly with minimum of rocking, and the exhaust is normal in its colouring.

When this point is reached the mixture strength can be checked by lifting the piston approximately 1·5 mm (0·062 in). To lift the piston use the special piston-lifting pin situated under the dashpot on the left-hand side of the carburetter. As the piston is lifted, the engine revolutions should increase very slightly. If the revolutions increase rapidly and continue to do so as the piston is raised further, the mixture is too rich and the jet-adjusting nut must be screwed *in* one flat and the mixture checked again in the same way. If the engine falters or stalls as the piston is raised its 1·5 mm, then the mixture is too weak and the jet nut must be screwed *down* one flat and the check carried out again.

The correct setting for the jet is when the engine revolutions increase *very* slightly as the piston is lifted, and then settle down to an even beat. However, do not hold the piston up for longer than 7 to 9 seconds. When the correct setting is reached, the throttle-adjusting screw—Fig. 23 (a)—can be set to give the tick-over speed required by the owner concerned, some prefer a fast idle speed whilst others prefer it quite slow.

A great deal of practice is needed to become expert at adjusting a carburetter successfully, so do not be-

19. Topping up carburetter damper oil well

Every 5 000 km (3 000 mile) intervals, unscrew the hexagon cap and fill the hollow piston rod with engine oil, refit the cap and damper. If this maintenance is not carried out regularly, the piston will fluctuate during acceleration and cause poor performance.

Also shown is the wing nut (arrowed), which secures the air cleaner in position.

20. Cleaning carburetter dashpot and piston (1)

Remove the dashpot and piston assembly after undoing the two screws which secure it to the body of the carburetter.

21. Cleaning carburetter dashpot and piston (2)

Clean the two outside diameters of the piston, the piston rod and the bore of the dashpot with rag moistened in petrol.

Assemble the parts when clean and dry, applying a few spots of light oil only to the piston rod. Do not forget to refill the damper reservoir after assembly.

22. Cleaning carburetter float chamber

This is not on the servicing schedules, but it may become necessary at some time.

Detach the float chamber by unscrewing the long bolt which attaches the chamber to the body of the carburetter. Note the nylon feed pipe disconnected from the float chamber.

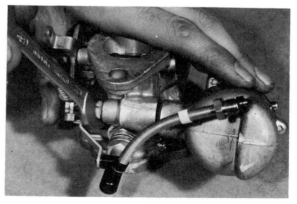

come dismayed if for the first few times you do not get it quite right. If the engine does not run properly after it has been adjusted, try again as set out above, and persevere until it runs correctly.

Carburetter faults and remedies

Below are listed some of the more common faults

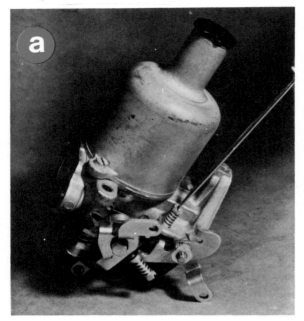

23. Adjusting SU HS2 carburetter

Showing points of adjustment. The procedure is fully explained in the text. The engine must be at normal running temperature. When the correct mixture of air and petrol is obtained at idling speed, the carburetter will produce the correct mixture at other engine speeds and throttle openings.

The fast-idle adjustment screw in photograph d controls the amount of throttle opening when the choke control is used for starting and fast-idle warming up. It should be set with a gap of about 1·6 mm ($\frac{1}{16}$ in) with the jet in the normal running position. If the position of jet-adjusting nut is altered substantially when adjusting the carburetter, the fast-idle screw may also need suitable readjustment.

(a) Engine speed is set by means of the throttle-stop adjusting screw.
(b) Mixture strength is adjusted by means of the jet-adjusting nut. This is screwed down to enrich and up to weaken the mixture.
(c) This shows the piston-lifting pin used for checking mixture-strength adjustment.
(d) The fast-idle adjustment screw indicated is part of the jet and throttle interconnection.

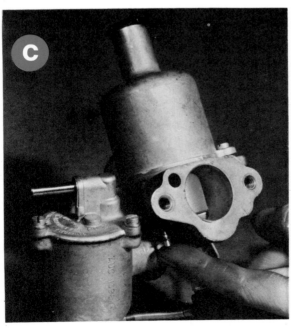

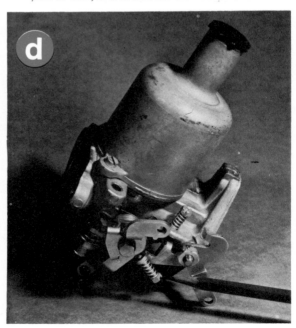

and the action that should be taken in each instance to rectify it.

(a) Difficult starting—This, of course, can be due to a great many things outside the fuel system but the first thing to check is always the ignition spark (as described under 'Difficult starting' in Chapter 7). If there is a good spark then turn to the carburetter. Check that the fuel is reaching the float chamber by disconnecting the feed pipe at the carburetter bowl, switching on the ignition momentarily, and seeing if petrol is pumped through. If there *is* fuel then remove the top of the float chamber and check that the needle valve is not stuck in the closed position (see below under Carburetter flooding). Shake the top vigorously a few times and replace it to see if petrol then reaches the carburetter.

If the fuel is reaching the bowl then a blocked jet in the carburetter is the next check, this is best left to a dealer as it involves dismantling the jet assembly completely and setting it up again in the right way. Should all these points be in order then the fault is not with the carburetter.

(b). Lack of power—If all the mechanical and ignition aspects of the engine are in order (e.g. plugs and points, ignition timing, no excess carbon present) then the carburetter needs tuning and the dashpot and piston require cleaning as detailed earlier.

(c) Popping, spitting and misfiring—Again this is more likely to be caused by faulty plugs, points, or ignition timing, but if they are all checked and found to be in order then make the same checks as in (a) because it is likely that there is fuel starvation.

(d) Carburetter flooding—Disconnect the feed pipe to the carburetter and remove the float chamber top. The operating fork for the needle valve can be seen and removed by withdrawing its fulcrum pin, whereupon the needle and seat assembly (the small brass hexagon-shaped unit in the bowl top) can be unscrewed and removed. On later models, the nylon float is attached to the fulcrum lever.

Thoroughly clean the needle and its seat and replace it, assembling the parts opposite to the way in which they were removed. If the unit still floods it means that a new needle-valve assembly is required as the old one is sticking somewhere, probably due to it being worn on one side more than the other.

(e) Stalling engine—Should the engine stall constantly every time the car comes to rest, then the slow-running may be set too low. Screw the throttle-adjusting screw down to speed up the tick-over and remove and clean the carburetter dashpot and piston. If the engine still stalls and refuses to idle, the carburetter probably needs a full tune as described earlier. If, after this, the fault is still present, the ignition, plugs, and points must be checked, cleaned, and reset.

AIR CLEANER
On both models, the air cleaner is of the renewable paper-element type, where the paper filter is impregnated with a chemical that causes dust and grit to adhere to its surface. Every 20 000 km (12 000 miles) the paper element should be discarded and a new one fitted.

By undoing the wing nut on the top of the air-cleaner casing (see Fig. 19), the top cover can be removed, thus exposing the paper element. Take this out and then detach the air-cleaner casing from the back of the carburetter completely. Wash the air-cleaner casing in petrol to remove all of the collected dirt from its interior and dry it thoroughly before re-attaching it to the rear of the carburetter. Place the new paper element inside and refit the lid, tightening down the wing nut securely.

FUEL-SYSTEM SECURING NUTS
Although it is not mentioned in the servicing schedules it is worthwhile taking the trouble during the 5 000 km (3 000 mile) service to check the tightness of the carburetter and manifold nuts and bolts. Do not try to tighten them further if they are already tight. Any slack ones should be tightened so as to obviate the risk of an air leak into the induction system, or a gas leak from the exhaust. At the same time check the tightness of all the securing clips on the pipes attached to the carburetter and fuel pump.

Chapter 6

Cooling and heating systems

The Clubman engine has a water cooling system of conventional design which also supplies the car's heater unit. The cooling system is pressurised and water circulation is assisted by a pump at the front of the engine and driven by the fan belt. From the bottom of the radiator, the water enters the cylinder block, circulates around the cylinders, combustion chambers, and valve ports, leaving the engine via the top hose and entering the radiator header tank. It then travels down the radiator tubes, being cooled by the passage of air through the radiator core, and reaches the bottom tank cooled and ready to enter the engine again.

The air is blown through the radiator by a fan attached to the water-pump drive pulley, this being driven by the fan belt.

The capacity of the cooling system, including heater, is 3·6 litres (6·25 UK pints). Information on the heating system is given at the end of the chapter.

RADIATOR PRESSURE CAP

A pressurised radiator-filler cap 0·91 kg/cm² (13 lb/in²) is fitted to the radiator. The effect of using a pressurised cap is to increase the boiling point of the cooling water. An internal-combustion engine becomes more efficient as its temperature increases and, provided the cooling water is not actually boiling, the hotter the water, the more efficient the engine. Should the cooling-water temperature exceed the higher boiling point, the pressure build up forces the pressure-release valve, attached to the radiator cap, off its seat and allows the water to pass through the radiator overflow pipe to atmosphere.

As the engine cools down, an atmospheric (vacuum-release) valve in the centre of the pressure-release valve is drawn off its seat. This allows air to enter the cooling system through the overflow pipe to prevent a partial vacuum being formed in the system.

Care should be taken when removing this type of radiator cap when the engine is hot. Although the

water may not be boiling, its temperature may be above normal boiling point and immediately the cap is released, the pressure on the cooling water is also released, which may cause boiling and personal injury. When removing the cap, turn it anti-clockwise very slowly if the engine is hot; this will gradually release the pressure.

THERMOSTAT

The wax-type thermostat is mounted in a circular housing at the front of the cylinder head. The radiator top hose is connected between the housing cover and the radiator header tank. To remove the thermostat for inspection and checking, partially drain the cooling system and disconnect the radiator top hose. Remove the radiator-cowling upper-support bracket. Unscrew the nuts and take off the thermostat cover from the studs. Remove the paper joint washer and lift out the thermostat.

A section through the AC wax-type thermostat is shown in Fig. 25. The thermostat is opened through

24. AC radiator pressure cap
1. *Pressure-release valve spring*
2. *Pressure-release valve*
3. *Vacuum release-valve spring*
4. *Expansion-chamber filler neck*
5. *Vacuum-release valve*

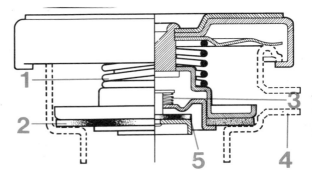

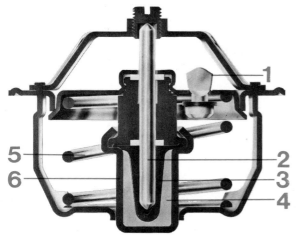

25. AC downward-opening wax-type thermostat

When replacing this type of thermostat, make sure the threaded stem faces upwards.

1. Jiggle pin
2. Piston
3. Rubber sleeve
4. Wax pellet
5. Spring
6. Cylinder

expansion of the wax pellet (4) in the cylinder (6) when melting due to heating, thus causing the cylinder to move away from the fixed piston (2).

The jiggle pin is fitted in the bleed hole, the object being to prevent any escape of water from the engine to the radiator through the valve bleed hole during rapid warm up. The jiggle pin is so constructed that when the engine is started, the pin is forced up by water-pump pressure and closes the bleed hole.

Checking thermostat
The standard-type thermostat used in the United

26. The radiator drain plug is located at the front end of the radiator bottom tank

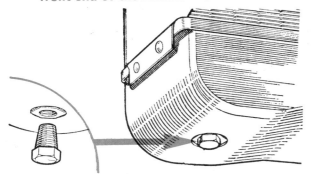

Kingdom opens at a temperature of 82°C (180°F). The opening temperature is marked on the thermostat.

To check the operation of the thermostat stand it in a container of water heated to the above temperature, when the thermostat should open fully in not less than one minute.

Any thermostat which does not operate satisfactorily must be replaced by a new unit. They cannot be repaired or adjusted. When replacing the thermostat in its housing, ensure that the unit is square and that a watertight joint is made between the cover and the housing: if necessary use a new ring gasket at this point.

ROUTINE MAINTENANCE
Apart from the weekly check on the water level in the radiator, the only other regular job that has to be done is the draining and flushing of the system before adding anti-freeze mixture. Remove the radiator filler cap and remove the two drain plugs, one at the bottom of the radiator and the other at the rear of the cylinder block, letting the old water run away completely.

Insert a hosepipe in the top of the radiator and run clean water through the system at a fairly fast rate until the water which runs out of the two drain points is seen to be quite clean. The drain plugs can then be refitted, and the system refilled with antifreeze.

LOSS OF WATER
Should the radiator require topping up at very frequent intervals it is quite obvious that there is a leak at some point and this must be found and rectified to obviate the risk of the car overheating, perhaps at an awkward time during a lengthy journey.

27. Location of cylinder-block drain plug or tap

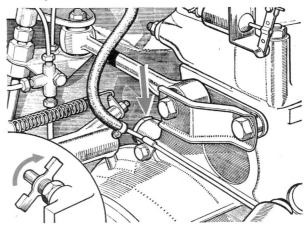

The starting place for this check is at the water hoses between the top and bottom of the radiator and engine. Firstly, tighten the clips which secure the hoses and then feel around the exterior of the pipes to see if they are wet, as sometimes water only seeps through the rubber very slowly. If they feel saturated new hoses are the only answer. New ones must be fitted by slackening off the clips as far as possible, pushing the hose along its junction with the engine and sliding it off the radiator end. The hose can then be pulled off the engine end and the new one fitted in the reverse procedure.

If the hoses and their clips are not faulty, inspect the two drain plugs. If they are leaking, new fibre washers are needed.

After checking all these points, if the loss is still apparent, the heater hoses must be looked at in the same way as for the radiator hoses. Tighten their clips, inspect for saturation and renew them if need be. If the heater radiator itself is leaking (not unknown, although quite rare), then this will soon be spotted as the water will drip on to the front carpet of the car. If this does happen a dealer will have to rectify it as it is quite a big job.

The only other point of exit for water is into the engine via a faulty cylinder-head gasket. This can be spotted by a fall-off in performance and water in the power-unit oil, or oil showing in the radiator top tank. A new cylinder-head gasket is the only remedy.

FAN BELT
Adjustment
The dynamo drive belt (fan belt) should have its tension checked every 10 000 km (6 000 miles). The tension is correct when there is about 13 mm (0·5 in) of free movement in the centre of the longest side of the belt. It must, of course, be tight enough to prevent slip, but not too tight, or undue strain is thrown on the dynamo front bearing. Where the tension needs adjustment, this must be carried out as follows:

Slacken the two nuts and bolts that attach the dynamo to the engine and also the two under the front of the dynamo which fit through a slotted lever. When all four are slack, with one hand pull the dynamo away from the engine so that it pivots about the top fixing bolts, until the desired tension is reached. Holding it there, use the other hand to tighten the large nut in the centre of the slotted lever. This will lock the dynamo in position and the other fixing nuts can then be tightened.

Removing fan belt
Should the fan belt ever need replacement, then the dynamo nuts and bolts must be slackened as above and the dynamo pushed as close as possible to the engine. Manoeuvre the belt off the dynamo pulley, then off the crankshaft pulley and finally over the fan

28. Slackening dynamo locating bolts for fan-belt adjustment

blades and remove it from the radiator cowling at the top right-hand corner where provision is made for this. The new belt must be fitted in the reverse procedure. A screwdriver or lever must *not* be used to force the belt over the dynamo pulley otherwise it may well crack. The owner's fingers must be employed to roll the belt on to the pulley.

One final warning is that when the fan belt is being adjusted, do not over-tighten it or excess wear will take place on the front dynamo bearing due to the strain being put on it. This will mean a costly repair bill or perhaps a reconditioned unit.

WATER PUMP
This is of the centrifugal impeller type and it is mounted on the front of the engine, being held in place by four bolts. The centre spindle of the pump, which runs right through it, has the impeller at one

29. Showing recess in radiator cowling to facilitate fan-belt removal

end and the flange for the fan blades at the other end and is sealed against entry of water by means of a spring-loaded carbon washer. To renew this washer will require the removal and dismantling of the pump and it is quicker and maybe cheaper in the long run to buy a British Leyland reconditioned unit.

No routine maintenance is required to the water pump. The pump has a sealed-for-life pre-lubricated bearing. Should the pump become extremely noisy or begin to leak at any time, then there is no alternative but to fit a factory-reconditioned unit available from any British Leyland dealer.

ANTI-FREEZE SOLUTIONS

Anti-freeze should always be used in winter, and must be used where a heater is fitted, as the heater unit cannot be drained.

There are various proportions of anti-freeze to water required to protect the engine down to different degrees of frost. To give protection down to $-13°C$ ($7°F$), 0·85 litre (1·5 UK pints) of anti-freeze is needed; to $-19°C$ ($-2°F$), 1·14 litres (2 UK pints) is needed; to $-36°C$ ($-33°F$), 1·85 litres (3·25 UK pints) is needed.

As relatively high temperatures are reached in the system, it is important that only anti-freeze of the ethylene-glycol type is used. Do *not* use an alcohol-based solution as these are unsuitable due to their high evaporation rate. The manufacturers recommend the use of Bluecol Anti-freeze (non-corrosive) or any solution which conforms to Specification BS 3151 or BS 3152. To add the anti-freeze, follow the procedure set out below.

Drain the cooling system completely as described earlier and flush it out thoroughly. Refit the drain plugs and check every hose clip, including those on the heater pipes, both under the bonnet and inside the car, for tightness. Fill the cooling system with approximately 1·7 litres (3 UK pints) of clean, fresh water and then pour in the requisite amount of anti-freeze, finally topping up the system with more water. Start the engine and run it at a fast idle speed until it is quite warm and the solution has had time to work its way around the system. Switch off the engine and make a final check to see that all the hose connections are satisfactory.

The reason that so much importance is credited to the hoses and pipes is that the anti-freeze has a searching effect and it will soon find any points of exit from the system, or entry to the engine. If a leak becomes apparent during the anti-freeze season, it is important that it is corrected as soon as possible as continual topping up of the radiator with water will weaken the mixture in the system, thus incurring further expense when more solution has to be introduced in order to give adequate protection.

One other point is that as water mixed with anti-freeze expands more than plain water, it is wise when topping up to do so only when the engine is hot, otherwise, when the engine heats up much of the mixture will be lost through the overflow pipe.

COOLING SYSTEM CLEANERS

Several firms which manufacture anti-freeze also make cleaners for the cooling system which can be used after the winter to ensure that all traces of anti-freeze and any sediment is cleaned out in readiness for the warmer weather.

When using these solutions follow the maker's instructions for the best results.

COOLING-SYSTEM FAULTS AND REMEDIES

There are only two complaints which have not already been covered, these being overheating and overcooling.

Overheating

The best way to cover this complaint is by setting out a list of points to check as there are several possible causes. It is up to the individual owner to decide whether he can make the repair or let a dealer carry out the work.

1. Low water level in the system—If overheating occurs this should always be the first check. Look for and correct any leaks and refill the cooling system in the prescribed way.

2. Broken or loose fan belt—This will become obvious by the ignition warning light staying on all the time as the dynamo will not be charging.

3. Broken or faulty filler cap on the radiator—This stops the system from becoming pressurised and drops the boiling point of the coolant.

4. Blocked water passages due to an accumulation of sediment in the system—To overcome this, flush out the system as described earlier.

5. Blocked radiator core due to an accumulation of mud and/or leaves under the wing—Keep this part of the underside of the body clear at all times.

6. Faulty thermostat—Jammed in the closed position. A wax-type thermostat is specified for these engines and if it becomes faulty, it normally jams in the shut position. This is opposite to the earlier bellows-type thermostat (containing methyl alcohol, water and a partial vacuum), which is basically naturally open and when it goes wrong, it fails safe in the open position.

These are the main causes of overheating that apply only to the cooling system, but some of the faults listed in Chapter 4 under 'Lack of Power' will also give rise to this complaint; for example, incorrect ignition timing, wrong carburetter mixture strength, incorrect valve rocker gaps, and excessive deposits of carbon in the combustion chambers.

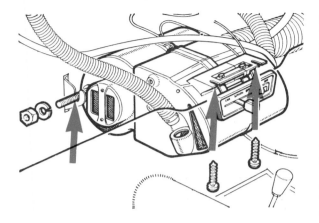

30. Heater fixing points
The arrows indicate the securing points for the heater under the facia.

Overcooling

When an engine does not reach its normal running temperature it is said to be running cool and quite often there is little that can be done as it is a feature of the engine concerned. The unit employed in Mini models is not known to suffer from this, so if the engine does not reach its normal running temperature there is probably something wrong. Of course, in the winter engines take much longer to get hot, and sometimes if the weather is really cold they do not get properly hot at all.

When this is the case a thermostat with a higher opening temperature can be fitted for the cold weather and a muff fitted to the front grille to stop the passage of cold air over the engine. If, by some twist, an engine does not get hot enough even in the warmer months, again, a different thermostat can be fitted to raise the temperature of the engine before water circulation takes place, but also have the carburetter mixture strength checked.

If there is too rich a mixture, a surplus of fuel is getting into the cylinders and not all of it is getting burned. Some of the fuel runs down the walls of the cylinders and with unburned fuel in the combustion chambers the flame spread is not as it should be, so that normal running temperature cannot be achieved.

HEATING AND DEMISTING UNIT

The heating system on the Clubman and 1275GT is of the 'fresh air' type where air is picked up from outside the car, passes via a large-diameter hose to the back of the heater radiator, is heated as it passes through the heater unit, and issues forth into the car interior from the underside of the facia parcel shelf. As the cars have wind-up windows with no separate quarter-lights, interior ventilation is by adjustable ducts situated at the extreme outside ends of the facia shelf; these ducts can be set to allow varying amounts of air to pass through by twisting the centre knob, and directed where required, by moving the duct in its mounting. For demisting purposes, the heater unit has pipes carrying air to vents along the underside of the windscreen.

The controls for the heater are located on a slide panel below the main switch panel on the facia lower rail. A single lever is moved along this slide to direct the air to the required area of the car interior, or to shut off air flow altogether.

The push-pull knob on the extreme right-hand side of the main switch panel is the temperature control; this controls a water valve and regulates the amount of hot water circulating through the heater. With the control knob pushed fully in, the maximum amount of heat is available; pulling out the knob will give a progressive reduction in temperature. On some cars, the heat-control knob is locked by turning it one-quarter turn clockwise; on these cars, do not move the control in or out whilst it is in the 'locked' position. On other models, the control needs no twisting; it locks itself in any position along the whole length of it travel.

For very cold conditions, or where the owner wishes to warm the car interior quickly, the heater has a booster fan. The switch for this is at the right-hand end of the heater slide panel and is a simple on-off control, the fan having only one speed.

As is common with most heater systems in modern cars, the actual heat is obtained by linking the heater radiator to the engine cooling system. At the rear of the cylinder head a control valve (which is connected to the push-pull knob on the facia) draws off hot water from the engine and circulates it through small-bore rubber pipes to the heater unit radiator; after passing through this it is taken back to the engine bottom hose via another small-bore pipe.

It must be remembered that when draining the cooling system, the heater radiator will not be completely drained, for although with the control knob pulled right out the heater is shut off from the rest of the cooling system, with the heater unit situated where it is, water remains inside it even when the engine water is drained away. This means that anti-freeze should always be used in the winter months, or if the car is to be laid up in cold weather; it will not be enough just to drain off the engine, as water inside the heater might still freeze.

There is no separate maintenance for the heater system, the routine laid down for the cooling system in general is quite enough. However, conscientious owners can check the hose clips and the condition of the hoses at the 10 000 km (6 000 mile) service, although it is very rare for them ever to need any attention.

SERVICING HEATER UNIT

Should a fault develop in the heater unit and it becomes necessary to replace a part, the following instructions will be found useful.

Removing heater assembly

Drain the cooling system and remove the front floor covering to avoid damage by coolant when disconnecting the heater pipes. Pull the demister and air-intake tubes out of the heater unit. Remove the two screws securing the front of the heater and slacken the nut securing the rear of the unit (see Fig. 30).

Disconnect the electrical connections from the

31. Components of the heater unit

1. *Blower motor*
2. *Rotor (air intake)*
3. *Rotor securing clips*
4. *Heater casing joining clips*
5. *Heater casing*
6. *Securing screws—control panel to casing*
7. *Blower switch*
8. *Heater control panel*
9. *Trunnion and screw—control lever to flap*
10. *Air-distribution flap*
11. *Matrix*
12. *Valve securing plate*
13. *One-way valve*
14. *Valve securing screws*
15. *Rotor (recirculatory)*

blower motor and switch. Then disconnect the heater water hoses, hold the fingers over the matrix pipes and lift the heater from the slotted rear bracket and out of the car. Drain the coolant from the heater.

Dismantling heater unit

Heater matrix replacement—Remove the blower switch/air-distribution panel (8), Fig. 31, (two screws), lever off the clips securing the twin casings (5) and separate the unit. Withdraw the matrix (11), clean the casings and fit the replacement unit.

Blower motor replacement—First remove the heater and take off the heater control panel (8), as described above. Then remove the motor assembly, withdraw each rotor from the unit and fit them to the replacement motor. Remove and connect the electrical wiring to the new unit. Refit the unit into the heater casing.

Blower switch replacement—The blower switch can be removed without removing the heater unit as follows: From behind the blower switch/air-distribution panel, pull off the electrical connections, and using a pair of pliers, press in the retainers on each side of the switch and manoeuvre the switch through the face of the panel. Press in the replacement switch and refit the electrical connections.

Refitting heater unit

Reverse the removal procedure and refill the cooling system. Start and warm up the engine, check for leaks and correct operation of the heater. Top up the coolant in the radiator to the correct level.

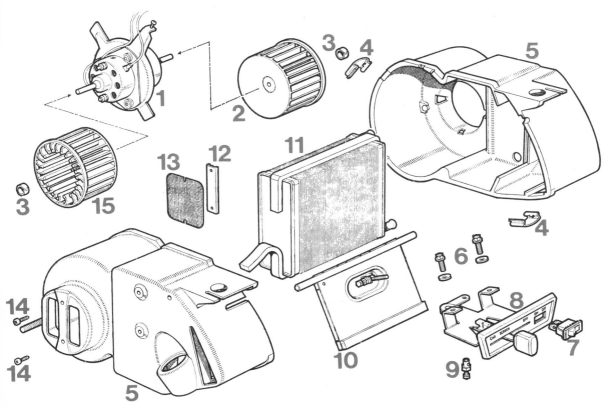

Chapter 7

Ignition system

There are two electrical circuits making up the ignition system, the primary and the secondary. The primary circuit comprises the battery, ignition switch, low-tension circuit of the coil, and the distributor contact points. In the secondary circuit are the high-tension circuit of the coil, the distributor rotor and cover segments, high-tension leads, and the spark plugs.

The battery is located in the luggage boot, under the mat, beside the spare wheel; it will be seen from the battery terminals that the polarity of the electrical system is negative ($-$) earth. In diagramatic form, the battery positive ($+$) terminal is connected through to the 'plus' terminal on the coil, to provide current to its primary winding.

The coil itself is mounted on the side of the engine adjacent to the distributor and has a weatherproof cover over its terminals. The 'minus' terminal of the coil is connected through to the side of the distributor

to provide the electrical feed to the contact-breaker points. From the centre of the coil a high-tension lead is connected to the distributor cap in order to transfer the high-voltage current to the rotor.

32. Ignition system
Circuit diagram showing the two circuits in the system—the primary (or low-tension) circuit and the secondary (or high-tension) circuit. The low-tension circuit is indicated by the thicker line. Note that the contact-breaker cam and rotor rotate in an anti-clockwise direction and the sparking plugs are connected to the distributor cap to give a firing order of 1, 3, 4, 2.
Note that when fitting a replacement coil, the contact-breaker lead must be connected to the ignition-coil terminal bearing the polarity sign of the battery earth post.

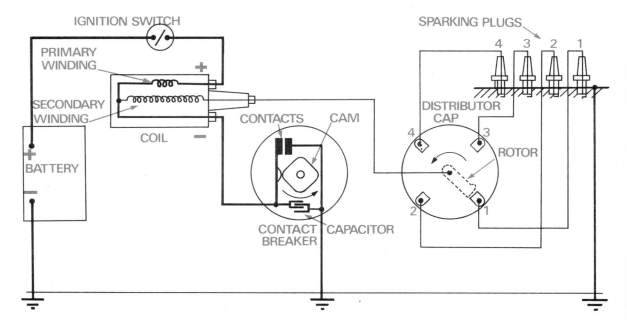

On the side of the engine facing the front of the car is the distributor, with a waterproof cover over its cap to prevent the leads shorting out. The distributor is fitted with both centrifugal and vacuum automatic ignition-advance mechanisms. Under the distributor cap is a baseplate assembly carrying the contact-breaker points and a capacitor (condenser), and through the centre of the baseplate protrudes a rotating cam which operates the points. On top of the cam is the rotor, which turns with the cam, passing as it does so the four segments in the distributor cap to which are connected the spark-plug high-tension leads.

OPERATION

When the ignition is switched on, the battery current flows through the primary circuit and a magnetic field is built up in the core of the coil. As the engine is turned (by the starter) the contact points are opened by their cam and the current flow is cut off suddenly. When this happens a very high voltage is induced in the secondary winding of the coil by the sudden collapse of the magnetic field.

This high-tension current is conveyed from the coil to the centre of the distributor cap via the high-tension cable between the two. It runs down the carbon brush to the rotor and, depending upon which segment the rotor is passing, it flows through to one of the spark plugs. This happens four times for every revolution of the distributor and each time the rotor is passing a different segment, thereby each plug in its correct turn is fed with the high-tension current and a spark jumps the plug gap, igniting the mixture in the cylinders.

It can be seen from this short description that the battery plays a very important part in the system. It is therefore imperative that it is kept in good condition by regular maintenance as set out in Chapter 13.

SERVICING SPARK PLUGS

Every 10 000 km ·(6 000 miles), the spark plugs should be removed, cleaned and reset, whilst at 20 000 km (12 000 miles) intervals they should be renewed. For the best possible performance from an engine, it is important that the spark plugs are maintained in good condition. In order to clean the plugs, remove the high-tension leads from the plugs, numbering them to ensure thay are put back correctly, and remove the plugs with a plug spanner and tommy bar. Naturally a high-pressure plug cleaner is the best possible way to remove all traces of carbon from the plugs, but a wire brush makes a good substitute, although it takes longer to get them perfectly clean.

Using a feeler gauge of 0·64 mm (0·025 in) thickness, set the gaps of the plugs by moving the side electrode *only*. Under no circumstances must the centre electrode be moved otherwise the porcelain insulating material will crack, rendering the plug useless. When all the plugs have been treated they can be refitted and the leads replaced. Do not forget to replace the washer to each plug before screwing it into the cylinder head.

When fitting new plugs, after removing them from their boxes, wash the electrodes in a little petrol to remove any grease that may have been applied by the makers for protection, then check the gaps as set out above before fitting them to the engine. All new plugs come with new washers so do not use the old ones which will have become flattened by constant use.

Fig. 33 shows a number of spark-plug conditions and also gives details of their possible causes. The correct plugs are Champion N5 or N9Y for Clubman and only N9Y for 1275GT models.

DISTRIBUTOR MAINTENANCE

Routine maintenance of the distributor is recommended every 10 000 km (6 000 miles). The attentions required are: (1) a checking operation of automatic advance-and-retard mechanisms; (2) checking condition of contact-breaker contacts; (3) adjusting breaker gap; and (4) lubricating the distributor.

To reach the parts of the distributor to be attended to, lift off the distributor cap after pulling aside the two spring clips, which hold the cap to the distributor body. Removal of the cap exposes the rotor mounted on the cam spindle in the centre of the assembly, and the contact-breaker assembly located around the cam.

Before servicing the distributor, turn the engine until the contact-breaker contacts are fully open— that is, with the heel of the contact-breaker lever on one of the peaks of the cam.

IGNITION ADVANCE-AND-RETARD MECHANISMS

For achieving good engine performance, the spark must be timed to arrive at each plug at the right instant in relation to the firing stroke of the piston in the cylinder. The best timing of the spark varies according to engine operating conditions and is the reason for incorporating automatic centrifugal and vacuum-timing mechanisms in the distributor. The centrifugal control varies the timing of the spark according to engine speed, while vacuum control varies timing according to the load on the engine.

Centrifugal timing control

The centrifugal-timing control is housed inside the distributor body. As engine speed increases above idling, the centrifugal mechanism advances the ignition—that is, it causes the spark to take place earlier. It does this by moving the cam round on its driving shaft in the same direction as the cam is rotated by the shaft, so that, as the engine speeds up, the contacts open earlier and, therefore, earlier sparking occurs. Below an engine speed of 800 rev/min, the centrifugal control produces no advance beyond the basic setting of ignition timing; the control produces maximum advance at 6 000 rev/min.

Vacuum timing control
The vacuum control varies timing automatically in response to the actual load placed on the engine. If the engine is not working hard (for example, when the throttle is eased back after acceleration), the vacuum control will pull the plate, upon which the contact-breaker assembly is mounted, round the cam in the opposite direction to that of cam rotation, causing the spark to occur earlier. When the throttle is opened for acceleration or going up a hill, the reverse action takes place—the plate moves back to retard the ignition. When the engine is idling, both centrifugal and vacuum controls are at full retard.

The vacuum unit is attached to the side of the distributor body and contains a flexible diaphragm. The chamber on one side of the diaphragm is connected, via a small pipe, to a tapping in the carburetter throttle bore. On its other side, the diaphragm is

33. Spark-plug conditions
(a) Normal condition—*Brown to greyish tan deposits and slight electrode wear, indicate correct spark-plug heat range and mixed periods of high- and low-speed driving. Spark plugs having this appearance may be cleaned, re-gapped and reinstalled.*

(b) Worn out—*Worn, eroded electrodes, and a pitted insulator are indications of 16 000 km (10 000 miles) or more of service. Spark plugs should be replaced when these conditions are observed for better fuel economy, quicker starting and smoother engine performance.*

(c) Carbon fouled—*Dry fluffy black carbon deposits may result from over-rich carburation, over-choking, or clogged air cleaner. Faulty breaker points, weak coil or condenser and worn ignition cables can reduce voltage and cause misfiring. Excessive idling, slow speeds under light load also can keep plug temperatures so low that normal combustion deposits are not burned off. In such a case a hotter type spark*

plug will better resist carbon deposits.

(d) Oil fouled—*Wet oily deposits may be caused by oil leaking past worn piston rings. 'Running-in' of a new or overhauled engine before rings are fully seated may also produce this condition. Excessive valve-guide clearances can also cause oil fouling. Usually these plugs can be degreased, cleaned and reinstalled. While hotter-type spark plugs will reduce oil-fouling, an engine overhaul may be necessary to correct this condition.*

(e) Burned electrodes—*Badly burned or eroded electrodes or burned or blistered insulator are indications of spark plug overheating. Improper spark (ignition) timing or low-octane fuel can cause detonation and overheating. Weak fuel/air mixtures, cooling-system stoppages or sticking valves may also produce this condition. Sustained high-speed, heavy-load service can lead to high temperatures which require use of colder spark plugs.*

a

b

c

d

e

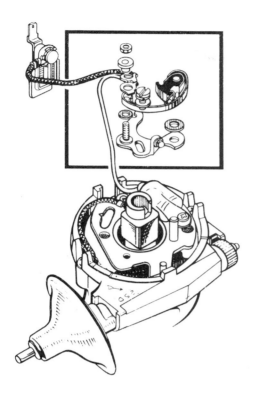

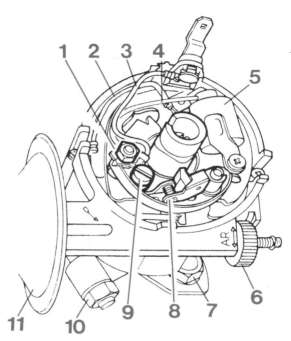

34. Exploded view of two-piece contact-breaker set

This type of contacts set can be replaced by the one-piece type. When assembling a two-piece set on the moving contact-breaker plate, which surrounds the cam, take care to use all the parts and to fit them in their correct order and position, as indicated above. Note that the small fibre insulating washer around the terminal post on the fixed-contact plate is positioned beneath the eye of the blade spring. The larger fibre insulating washer around the post upon which the contact-breaker lever pivots is placed between this lever and the fixed-contact plate.

35. Lucas 'Quikafit' one-piece contact-breaker set

36. Contact-breaker fitted with one-piece Lucas 'Quikafit' contacts set

The complete contacts set is removed for renewal or renovation after detaching nut (1) and leads (3 and 4) from the insulated post and unscrewing locking screw (9).

1. *Nut ensuring electrical connection between contact-breaker lever spring and leads on insulated terminal post*
2. *Earth lead from moving-contact-breaker plate to distributor body*
3. *Lead from low-voltage terminal of distributor*
4. *Low-voltage lead to capacitor*
5. *Capacitor*
6. *Micrometer timing adjuster*
7. *Distributor retaining bolt*
8. *Contact-breaker lever carrying moving contact*
9. *Screw for locking fixed-contact plate to moving contact-breaker plate*
10. *Distributor-body clamp-bolt*
11. *Vacuum timing-control unit*

linked to the moving contact-plate in the distributor. The diaphragm is spring-loaded in the direction of full retard so that increasing vacuum in the throttle bore draws the diaphragm against spring pressure to advance the ignition; decreasing vacuum causes the

spring to push the diaphragm back towards the fully-retarded position. Maximum advance given by the vacuum control is about 8° of plate movement around the cam, equivalent to 16° of crankshaft rotation.

Checking ignition-timing mechanisms

To check the centrifugal control, take hold of the rotor and rotate it in the direction of cam rotation (anti-clockwise), then release it. The rotor should return freely to its starting position. If not, dirt is likely to be obstructing movement and the mechanism needs cleaning. Cam movement for full advance is about 12°, which corresponds to 24° crankshaft rotation. The centrifugal mechanism, consisting of governor weights and springs, can be reached after lifting off the rotor, disconnecting the vacuum-control link on the rim of the moving contact-plate, removing this plate and then detaching the baseplate (secured by two screws) underneath.

To check the operation of the vacuum-timing control, push the moving contact-plate in a clockwise direction—that is, against normal direction of cam rotation. There is a certain amount of stiffness because the plate has to be moved against diaphragm-spring pressure; undue stiffness of movement indicates that the moving-plate bearing surfaces need cleaning.

SERVICING CONTACT-BREAKER CONTACTS

Checking the contacts is recommended as routine every 10 000 km (6 000 miles). It involves examination of the contacts for condition, then cleaning, or renovating, or renewing them, as found necessary, and finally checking and adjusting the gap between the contacts. Before checking the contacts, remove the rotor from the top of the cam by pulling it off upwards. The contact set consists of the fixed-contact plate and the lever which carries the moving contact.

The owner may decide to discard the existing contacts and replace them with a new set, or if the contacts are not too badly burnt, to reface them.

37. Distributor lubrication (1)

Pull the rotor from the top of the cam sleeve. Insert a few drops of oil to lubricate the cam bearing as shown. Lubricate the automatic ignition-advance mechanism by putting a drop or two of oil under the cam through the hole in the contact-breaker baseplate.

38. Distributor lubrication (2)

Lightly smear the cam surface with grease or engine oil. Also place a dab on the pivot of the contact-breaker lever.

tacts are not too badly burnt, to reface them.

After removing the contact set, clean up each contact face with a fine carborundum stone or fine emery cloth. Rub the contact back and forth on the abrasive, keeping the face level and square. Any build-up of metal on the face should be rubbed off. Discard the contact set if a contact face is badly pitted. After trimming up, wipe away any abrasive or metal particles with a petrol-moistened rag.

Removing and fitting contacts

The removal of contacts differs according to type, one-piece or two-piece. A two-piece contact set cannot be fitted where the 'Quikafit' one-piece set is original equipment, but a one-piece set can replace a two-piece set.

Two-piece contact set (Fig. 34)—To remove, first unscrew the small nut which anchors the eye end of the contact-breaker spring to a pillar on the fixed-contact plate. This allows the contact-lever assembly, with spring and moving contact, to be lifted from its pivot post and, at the same time, the spring eye to be detached, together with nylon insulating sleeve and two leads, from the pillar. Note the small fibre insulating washer fitted on the pillar below the spring eye. To remove the fixed-contact plate, undo the screw attaching it to the moving-contact plate.

When fitting the two-piece set, do not forget the large fibre insulating washer located under the contact lever on the lever-pivot post. Remember also to refit the small fibre washer under the spring eye. The lead terminals are located beneath the flange of the nylon sleeve so that they make contact with the spring eye. *One-piece contact set (Fig. 36)*—To remove the complete set, unscrew the nut from the insulated terminal pillar and undo the slotted screw securing the fixed-contact plate. To remove the moving-contact assembly only, leave the slotted screw in position and lift the spring eye from the terminal pillar and the contact lever from its pivot post.

When fitting the one-piece set, place the two electrical leads on the insulated terminal and thread the nut down on the terminal until the lead connections just press against the spring eye, then tighten the nut a further half-turn only.

DISTRIBUTOR LUBRICATION
With cap and rotor removed, the distributor mechanisms should be lubricated. Using an oilcan containing engine oil, insert a few drops into the centre of the cam spindle upon which the rotor fits (see Fig. 37) Do not remove the screw visible there, as the oil is able to run down between this and the cam to lubri-

39. The contact-breaker point gap should be checked and adjusted every 10 000 km (6 000 miles)
Turn the engine until the contacts are fully open— that is, with the contact-breaker lever on one of the peaks of the cam. Then measure the contact gap, as shown, with a feeler gauge—thickness 0·38 mm (0·015 in). If adjustment is necessary slacken the slotted screw which secures the fixed-contact plate and adjust the gap by inserting a screwdriver (as shown) in the notched hole in the plate, turning clockwise to decrease and anti-clockwise to increase the gap. The gauge should be a sliding fit in the gap. Do not forget to retighten the screw after adjusting the gap.

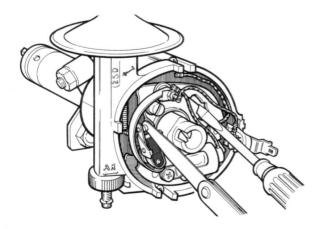

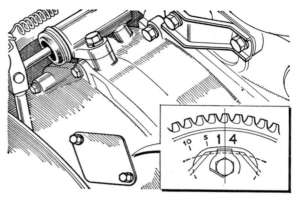

40. The cover plate on the flywheel housing and the markings that can be seen on the flywheel
1/4 is the top dead centre (tdc) position, but 5°, 10° and .15° positions before tdc are also given.

cate the cam bearing. Insert a few drops of oil in the aperture in the moving contact-plate around the cam; this oil will run down and lubricate the centrifugal-advance mechanism. Apply a light smear of grease to the post upon which the contact-breaker lever pivots. Finally, lightly smear the cam itself with a little grease; do not put on a lot of grease, as it will get thrown off on to the contacts and affect engine running. Wipe away all surplus oil and ensure that the contacts are perfectly clean.

CONTACT-BREAKER GAP ADJUSTMENT
After the above contact-breaker maintenance has been completed, the gap between the contacts, in their fully-open position, must be checked and adjusted as necessary (Fig. 39). Turn the engine over until the heel of the contact lever rests on one of the peaks of the cam, at which point the contacts will be fully open. One way of turning the engine is to jack up one front wheel, put the gearbox into top gear and then rotate the jacked-up wheel until the contacts are seen to be fully open.

Using a feeler gauge of 0·38 mm (0·015 in) thickness, check the gap. The gauge should be a sliding fit. If the gap is too wide or too narrow, it must be adjusted. Adjacent to the contacts is a slotted screw which secures the fixed-contact plate to the moving-contact plate. After slackening this screw, the fixed-contact plate can be moved until the required fully-open contacts gap is present. Notches in both plates allow a screwdriver to be inserted and twisted to move the fixed-contact plate in the required direction. When the gap is correct, the screw can be tightened and the gap checked again after tightening to be sure it is still correct.

INSPECTING IGNITION COMPONENTS

There are no other set jobs in the servicing schedule for the ignition system, but one or two other items may need attention. Periodically, a complete inspection should be made of the distributor, high-voltage leads and ignition coil.

Distributor

Check the tightness of the cable connections to distributor and coil. Give the distributor cap a thorough clean inside and out. Inspect it closely to ascertain that it is not cracked or chipped, or has 'tracking' lines on its surface, indicating high-voltage leakage paths (see under 'Test for voltage at plugs' later in this chapter).

Using a sharp penknife, scrape any accumulated deposit from the metal terminal electrodes inside the cap, to which the plug leads are connected. At the same time, give the metal part of the rotor a good clean to ensure that there is no interference with current flow as the rotor goes past the terminal electrodes at high speed. Check that the rotor moulding is not cracked or has tracking marks on its surface.

Check the carbon brush that makes contact with the top of the rotor. It is lightly spring-loaded in the distributor cap and it can be gently pulled down slightly to make sure that it is pressing down sufficiently on the rotor when the cap is in place. When doing this, however, do not pull down too hard otherwise it may well come right out of its holder.

Checking high-voltage leads

The high-voltage leads can be inspected next. If their insulation covering is in poor condition, leakage of voltage from the leads to nearby metal could take place and result in inferior ignition performance.

Suppression-type cables are used, the cable conductor being a cord material, such as silk, impregnated with graphite, giving it sufficient electrical resistance to suppress interference with car-radio reception. Replacement high-tension leads can be obtained complete with sound terminal connections on the cable ends. Making up your own leads from resistive cable requires practice, a special crimping tool, and a supply of suitable staples and terminal straps.

Checking coil

There is no set servicing procedure for the ignition coil but, as with the distributor, it is a good idea to make a periodical check on its condition and the tightness of its cable connections. The low-voltage terminals can be disconnected and inspected for any signs of corrosion and, if some is seen, the terminal surfaces should be cleaned and then treated with a little petroleum jelly before being reconnected. While the cables are disconnected, the top of the coil can be wiped clean to remove any traces of dirt or grease.

IGNITION TIMING

If ever the ignition timing is lost, perhaps due to the distributor clamp coming loose, then it will have to be reset accurately before the engine will run efficiently. Having described earlier how the spark is transferred to each plug in turn, it can be seen that the spark must arrive at each plug at exactly the right time, that is when the piston is nearing top dead centre (tdc) of the compression stroke.

In order that this may happen, the engine designers lay down a firing order for the cylinders when the engine is in its early stages of design; in the case of these cars the firing order is 1, 3, 4, 2 which means that if the ignition timing is set on No. 1 cylinder, the next one that fires will be No. 3, then No. 4, then No. 2. This firing order should always be known if the leads from the distributor cap to the plugs are ever removed or mixed up, for they can quite simply be replaced by fitting a lead to No. 1 plug, then following the firing order sequence around the segments (keeping to the direction of rotation of the rotor) and fitting the other leads.

Resetting the timing

To reset the ignition timing follow this procedure: Rotate the engine (see under 'Rotating the engine' in Chapter 4) until No. 1 cylinder (the one nearest the fan blades) has its piston at tdc on its firing stroke. This can be ascertained by removing the rocker cover from the engine and watching the valves; when the valves for No. 4 cylinder are 'rocking' (i.e. exhaust valve just closing and inlet just opening) No. 1 piston is nearing tdc on its firing stroke.

At the rear of the engine is a small diamond-shaped cover plate on the flywheel housing, remove this and by using a small mirror to see through the aperture, the flywheel can be seen. Having reached the stage above with No. 4 cylinder valves on the rock, the timing marks on the flywheel should be in the region of the aperture. Rotate the engine slowly until the 1/4 mark on the flywheel is lined up exactly with the pointer attached to the housing. The piston is then at tdc (top dead centre) and the engine can be turned back from this position until the correct degree setting before tdc is reached.

For the Clubman, the correct setting should be at 5° before tdc and with the 1275GT, 8° before tdc. On the flywheel there are markings for both 5° and 10° before the 1/4 mark so it is quite a simple matter to get the engine set at exactly the right point.

On automatic-transmission cars, the same procedure as above can be employed, but the engine should be turned by inserting a screwdriver through the aperture in the converter housing (adjacent to the oil dipstick) and levering the starter ring gear. The timing marks can be seen stamped on the converter after removing the cover to the aperture.

41. Ignition timing
For final ignition setting, the knurled nut shown is turned as required. To retard the ignition the nut must be turned clockwise, and anti-clockwise to advance the ignition. The knurled nut 'clicks' 55 times at each graduation on the scale and as each graduation represents 5° of timing, it can be seen that 11 clicks alters the timing by 1°.
The clamp-bolt indicated is used to make the initial ignition-timing setting. It secures the distributor body to the engine and, when slackened, allows the distributor to be turned round the cam—clockwise to advance and anti-clockwise to retard.

The setting for automatics should be 4° before tdc.

With the engine thus set, attention should now be transferred to the distributor. Slacken the distributor-body clamp-bolt (indicated by pencil in Fig. 41) and rotate the distributor body anti-clockwise until the contact points can be seen to be fully closed, then slowly turn it in a clockwise direction until the points just.commence to open. Stop there and tighten the clamp. Offer up the distributor cap to make sure that the rotor is adjacent to the segment in the cap for No. 1 plug lead and if so put it to one side whilst the contact points are set with the correct gap as described earlier in this chapter.

Replace the distributor cap (not forgetting the rotor) and connect the distributor wire, and replace all spark-plug leads in their correct order. Finally, connect the vacuum-advance pipe to the distributor.

Refit the cover to the flywheel housing and your engine should now be correctly timed for starting. Final adjustment to the timing can be made during a road test by using the ratchet-type knurled adjusting nut on the side of the distributor (Fig. 41); it is possible when lining up the timing marks on the flywheel to be slightly out on the accurate setting,

so this 'fine tuner' of the ignition timing is provided.

It is really best to make the final setting using a stroboscopic light or by connecting the car to an electronic tuner, then the actual timing at running speed can be seen. When using the adjusting nut on the distributor it must be turned clockwise to retard the ignition and anti-clockwise to advance it. Each graduation on the scale is equivalent to 5° of timing movement and there are 55 clicks on the adjuster, so remember that 11 clicks equal 1°. Having set the ignition properly as described above, the final tuning should not involve more than 7 or 8 clicks on the adjuster either way to get the engine at a perfect setting.

DISTRIBUTOR REMOVAL AND REFITTING
The distributor is rotated at half engine speed by a hollow drive shaft which is itself rotated by skew gear from the crankshaft. Attached to the end of the distributor driving spindle is a dog which engages in a slot in the top end of the drive shaft. As the slot is slightly offset, the lobe on one side of the slot is larger than the other. When the engine is set with the 1/4 mark on the flywheel in the centre of the aperture and No. 1 piston firing, the drive-shaft slot is at the 2 o'clock position with the larger lobe uppermost.

Before removing the distributor, turn the engine to the 1/4 mark on the flywheel, with the distributor rotor pointing in the direction of No. 1 plug-lead terminal in the cap. Disconnect the low-voltage lead from the contact-breaker terminal and the vacuum pipe from the distributor vacuum unit. Undo the two fixing-plate bolts holding the distributor to the engine and withdraw the distributor upwards.

Replace the distributor with the engine markings and drive-shaft slot in the same positions.

IGNITION FAULTS AND FAULT TRACING
Most of the ignition faults causing difficult starting, misfiring or loss of power have already been mentioned, for to prevent them is the object of routine maintenance.

In general, deterioration in the ignition system shows up more when starting the engine than in normal running. In turning a cold engine, the starter motor takes a large current from the battery and this tends to rob the primary ignition circuit of some of the voltage needed for inducing the high-voltage spark. Such voltage drop is of little consequence when the ignition system is in shape. When the battery is in a low state of charge or poor condition, then its voltage drop increases. Additional voltage drop also occurs when battery or starter connections are not tight.

Here is a simple test procedure for finding out whether the ignition system is responsible for starting difficulty, misfiring or lack of power and how to locate and deal with the cause. The method assumes that the battery is able to turn the starter over at normal speed.

FAULT LOCATION
Checking secondary circuit
The purpose of the first stage of the test procedure outlined below is to find out whether high voltage is reaching the distributor.

At its distributor end disconnect the high-voltage lead between coil and distributor cap. Hold the lead with its end about 6 mm ($\frac{1}{4}$ in) away from a clean point on the engine cylinder block or head whilst the engine is turned over on the starter motor. If sparking at the lead end is good, it confirms that the ignition system is operative up to this point. Consequently, the trouble must be in the spark plugs or in the high-voltage distribution arrangements between the distributor-cap centre terminal and the spark plugs.

Test for voltage at plugs
In the above event, the next step is to find out whether voltage is reaching the spark plugs. Reconnect the coil lead to the distributor cap. Carry out a spark test, this time on a plug lead detached from one of the plugs and held 6 mm ($\frac{1}{4}$ in) from the cylinder head. Each plug lead may be tested in turn. If the sparking is strong and regular across all plug lead gaps, then the trouble is with the plugs and they must be removed for inspection, cleaning and re-gapping, or renewing.

If there are plug leads from which no spark or only a weak irregular spark is emitted, the trouble lies either (a) in the poor conditions of the plug leads, or (b) in the distributor cap, the trouble here being associated with faulty distribution of voltage from the brush and rotor to the plug-lead terminal electrode or electrodes in the cap.

Examine the plug lead concerned and if any faults are found, renew the cable. Remove and clean the distributor cap. Inspect its surfaces, noting whether there is 'tracking' indicated by a thin black line on the moulding surface between plug-lead terminal electrodes or between an electrode and the rim of the cap. If there is such tracking or any cracks in the moulding, it will be necessary to replace the cap with a new one. See that the brush is not sticking in the cap. Examine the rotor for cracking or tracking over its moulding and the rotor metal electrode for excessive wear.

After replacements have been made, the engine can be started up to see if the trouble has been cured; attention to spark plugs may still be needed.

Checking primary circuit
If there is no spark during the coil-lead spark test, or only a weak irregular spark, the next step is to check whether the fault is in the low-voltage primary circuit.

To test whether battery voltage is reaching the contact-breaker feed terminal, detach the lead from the terminal and connect a test bulb between the end of the lead and the body of the distributor. (A suitable test bulb is a 12-volt 2·2 watt warning lamp). Switch on the ignition.

If the test bulb lights, supply voltage is reaching the contact-breaker terminal and the trouble is obviously located either in the contact breaker or in the secondary (high-voltage) circuit.

Therefore, check the contact-breaker parts by inspection, test, or replacement. The condition of the contacts can be observed. If defective, the contacts should be refaced or replaced. The contact-points gap should be checked and adjusted. Internal wiring continuity can be checked by placing the test lamp in series between the lead and the contact-breaker terminal (with the points closed). A defective capacitor (condenser) can cause misfiring or ignition failure. Frequent burning of contacts is an indication of a failing capacitor but in the absence of special test equipment, a capacitor can be checked only by substituting it for one known to be sound and judging by the result.

After putting right any defect found in the contact-breaker assembly, the secondary (high-voltage) circuit can be tested by means of the coil-lead spark test described earlier.

If it is found when checking the primary circuit, that there is no voltage at the contact-breaker feed terminal, remove the lead from the negative (−) terminal of the ignition coil. Connect the test bulb between this terminal and earth. If the bulb lights, the wire from coil '−' terminal to the contact-breaker terminal must be broken.

If the bulb does not light when connected between the coil '−' terminal and earth, it indicates a fault in the wiring from the ignition switch, or in the primary winding of the ignition coil. To trace the fault, connect a jumper lead (i.e. a length of cable) in parallel with the lead between ignition switch and coil + terminal and test with the bulb between coil + terminal and earth. If the bulb lights, there is a fault in the primary winding of the coil. If the bulb does not light, there is a discontinuity in the wiring from the switch. This can be confirmed by by-passing the ignition switch and its associated wiring. Connect a jumper lead between battery + and coil + terminals. The test bulb connected between coil + terminal and earth should then light.

Chapter 8

Braking system

Both the Clubman and 1275GT cars are fitted with Lockheed braking systems, but that is where the similarity ends; the Clubman has drum brakes all round, these being 178 mm (7 in) diameter and having two-leading shoes at the front and one lead-ing, one trailing at the rear. The 1275GT has 190-mm (7.5-in) diameter disc brakes at the front and 178-mm (7-in) diameter drum brakes at the rear, and is power-assisted by a Lockheed Type 6 servo unit.

The master cylinder is situated under the bonnet attached to the bulkhead and on later models is a tandem unit such that the hydraulic circuit for the front and rear brakes are independent of each other; therefore if a failure occurs in one circuit, at least the car will not be devoid of brakes completely.

Steel piping takes the brake fluid from the master cylinder to the four wheels, the final length to the actual brake operating cylinders being of flexible piping to allow for wheel and suspension movement. Inserted in the hydraulic pipeline to the rear wheels is a regulator valve which limits the pressure to the rear-wheel cylinders; this is necessary to combat the uneven front-to-rear weight distribution of the Mini cars.

The handbrake operates on the rear brakes only, the lever being positioned between the front seats where its lower end connects to two cables which run via trunnions to each rear-brake backplate. There they connect up with short levers that pass through the backplate and work directly against the brake shoe.

OPERATION

The working principle is quite straightforward; when the brake pedal is depressed, the master-cylinder pistons are pushed along their bores to pressurise the hydraulic pipelines. The fluid pressure is felt behind the pistons in the wheel cylinders and are forced out, in turn, forcing the brake shoes against their drums thus slowing their rotation.

With disc front brakes a similar principle is em-ployed. The pistons in the front caliper assemblies are forced out, pushing the brake pads ahead of them, thereby causing them to grip the disc and slow its movement.

The servo unit produces increased hydraulic pres-sure without a similar increase in pressure on the part of the driver's foot. What happens is that as the brake pedal is depressed, and the hydraulic lines are pressurised, after a set amount of pedal travel, a valve is uncovered in the servo which causes a vacuum to

42. Location of brake and clutch master cylinders in engine compartment

Note that the correct fluid level is marked on the side of the brake reservoir. The level of fluid in the clutch reservoir should be kept to the bottom of the filler neck. On earlier models, the brake master cylinder is of similar shape to the clutch master cylinder.
1. Tandem-type brake master cylinder
2. Brake fluid reservoir cap
3. Clutch master cylinder
4. Clutch fluid reservoir cap

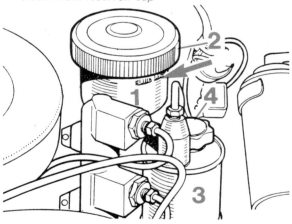

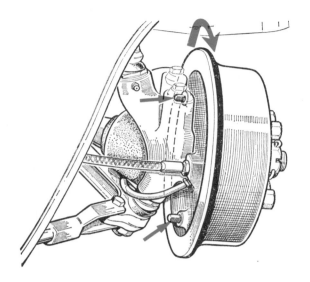

43. Front-wheel brake adjustment—Clubman models
Showing the two square-headed screws on each front wheel used for adjusting the brake shoes. Each adjuster is turned in the direction of wheel rotation to bring the brake shoe nearer the drum. Self-adjusting disc brakes are used on 1275GT cars.

be felt behind the servo piston, which in turn moves it along its cylinder with tremendous force and as it is connected through to the hydraulic brake lines it pressurises the system at a higher rate than the driver could by foot pressure alone, giving extra-powerful braking.

ROUTINE MAINTENANCE
At 5 000 km (3 000 mile) intervals, the following checks and adjustments should be made:

Topping up brake fluid
Inspect and top up if necessary the brake fluid in the master-cylinder reservoir. This is situated under the bonnet on the right-hand side of the bulkhead, looking from the driver's seat (Fig. 42). Wipe the top of the reservoir until every trace of dirt and grease has disappeared then unscrew the cap.

The level of the fluid should be up to the mark indicated on the outer casing of the reservoir, which is approximately 13 mm (0·5 in) below the top lip of the reservoir. If it is below this level, then bring it up to the mark by adding British Leyland UNIPART 410 or 550 Brake Fluid to the Clubman cars; with the 1275GT use only the UNIPART 550 fluid as this mixture has a higher boiling point, suitable for disc brakes. An alternative fluid for all models is Lockheed 329S Universal Brake Fluid.

After topping up, replace the reservoir cap securely and make sure that its breather hole is clear.

When pouring the brake fluid, the owner must be careful not to spill any on the car's paintwork as it will cause irreparable damage to the paint surface.

Adjusting brakes for wear
On the Clubman models, both the front and rear brakes have to be adjusted, whereas the front disc brakes of the 1275GT are self-adjusting, so with these models only the instructions applying to the rear brakes should be followed.
Front-drum brakes—Check the brake-pedal travel. If the movement is excessive before the brakes come on, then it means the brake linings have worn and to rectify this a simple adjustment has to be made to bring the brake shoes nearer their drums.

Jack up the front of the car and place supports under the sub-frame. Lie under the car behind one of the wheels and on looking at the brake backplate, square-headed screws will be seen protruding from the top and bottom. Taking one of these adjusters at a time, screw it in the same direction as the forward

44. Location of the rear-brake adjuster at the top of the backplate
There is only one adjuster on each rear brake. On both wheels, the adjuster is turned clockwise to bring the brake shoes nearer the drum.

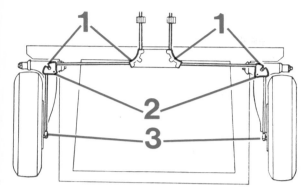

45. Lubrication points for the handbrake cables that run around the rear-suspension trailing arms

1. *Cable guides (grease)*
2. *Pivot pins for swinging sectors (oil)*
3. *Handbrake-lever clevis pins on brake backplate (grease)*

rotation of the front wheel until the wheel is locked solid. Then slowly let it off until the wheel just turns freely without the brakes rubbing. Do the same with the other adjuster and the adjustment is complete for that wheel; move to the other front wheel and employ the same procedure. ·

Rear-drum brakes—Having let down the front of the car, the rear wheels can be raised and supports placed under the sub-frame. Check that the handbrake is let off, then follow the same instructions as given for the front brakes, except that there is only one adjuster on each rear brake and both adjusters are turned clockwise to lock the wheel.

Handbrake adjustment

Under normal circumstances, the handbrake is automatically adjusted when the rear brakes are adjusted. However, if after the rear brakes have been adjusted the handbrake lever still has a movement of more than five 'clicks' on its ratchet then it requires separate adjustment.

Jack up the rear of the car and pull on the handbrake three 'clicks'. At the base of the handbrake lever, the threaded ends of the two cables pass through a trunnion and brass nuts secure them in place. With the lever set at three 'clicks', screw the brass nuts further along the threaded ends of the cables; do this on each cable until the rear wheels can just be turned under heavy hand pressure, and get as near as possible to the same amount of force needed to turn each rear wheel.

Let off the handbrake lever completely to make sure that the wheels are free to turn and the shoes are not rubbing on the drums. The handbrake is then correctly set.

The following service attentions are required every 10 000 km (6 000 miles):

Handbrake linkage lubrication

On all models, the two handbrake cables run from the bottom of the lever to the two rear wheels. They run down the underside of the car each side of the exhaust system, make a right-angle turn through two guide channels on the rear sub-frame, make a further right-angle turn around two swinging sectors, then attach to the levers in the brake backplates.

If left to their own devices these cable guides and sectors soon seize up due to their exposure to the elements under the car, quite often giving rise to the rear brakes hanging on or the handbrake not working. This can be avoided by regular cleaning and lubrication. At the mileage stated above take a wire brush and clean all accumulated dirt and grease off the cable guides and swinging sectors; make sure the latter are free to swing on their pivots.

Smear grease into and around the cable guides on the sub-frame and into the parts of the sectors where the cables run. Lubricate the sector pivots with an oilcan. Smear a little grease around the clevis

46. Front disc brake—1275GT cars

1. *Pad retaining pins*
2. *Brake pads*
3. *Anti-squeak shims*
4. *Bleed valve*

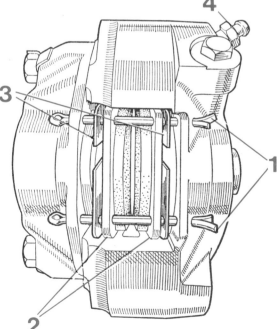

pin through the attachment for each cable to the short lever on the brake backplate.

Finally operate the handbrake lever a few times to work the lubricant into the system.

Inspecting brake disc and pads for wear—1275GT cars

Jack up the front of the car and remove the road wheels. Looking in from the back of each caliper unit, the disc pads can be seen and the amount of lining material left on each of them gauged. When the linings are down to their minimum allowed thickness of 1·6 mm (0·062 in), they must be changed for a new set, for if the lining material is allowed to wear down to the metal then the disc will get badly scarred.

Across the aperture at the back of each caliper unit are two long split-pins which pass through the caliper body and also through the pads to locate them. Remove both the pins and the old pads can be withdrawn from each side of the caliper with a pair of pliers. Using a long screwdriver, or a tyre lever, insert it between the disc and the piston in the

caliper unit and press the piston back into its bore, repeat this on the other side of the caliper.

The two new pads can then be slipped into place and the split-pins reinserted. Exactly the same treatment is required at the other front wheel to renew the pads. If there are any thin, flat shims fitted behind the pads in the caliper, then these have to be refitted in exactly the same way to the new pads—they are anti-squeak shims and to leave them out could give rise to noisy brakes.

Once the new pads are fitted to both sides, check the level of the brake fluid in the master-cylinder reservoir, then pump the brake pedal a few times until it gets hard. By doing this, the front brakes are automatically adjusting themselves and no further adjustment is required. The front wheels can then be replaced and the job is complete.

There is a word of warning in respect to this particular job, having removed the old pads, before levering the pistons back into the caliper make sure there is some old rag wrapped around the neck of the

47. Components of Lockheed left-hand front-drum brake—Clubman models
1. *Brake cylinders*
2. *Trailing end of brake shoes*
3. *Leading end of brake shoes*
4. *Shoe-return springs*
5. *Spring-loaded hooks (retaining tips of brake shoes to wheel-cylinder pistons)*

48. Components of Lockheed right-hand rear-drum brake—all models
1. *Double-acting brake cylinder*
2. *Handbrake lever*
3. *Brake shoes*
4. *Adjuster*
5. *Shoe-return springs*
Using a double-acting wheel cylinder gives leading/trailing-shoe characteristics in both directions of wheel rotation.

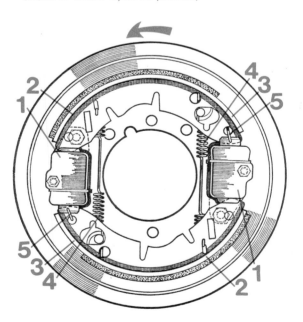

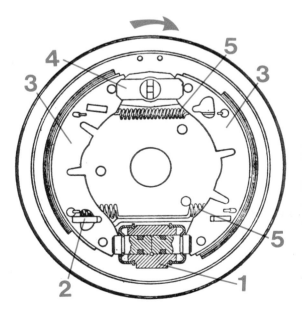

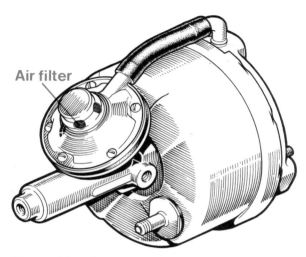

Air filter

49. Lockheed vacuum-servo unit fitted to 1275GT cars
The air-valve cover should be removed and the filter chamber cleaned using a low-pressure air-line every 20 000 km (12 000 miles).

master-cylinder reservoir. As the pistons are pushed back into the caliper body, the hydraulic fluid is forced back along the pipes and if the master cylinder is full some fluid will overflow; if this gets onto the car paintwork it can damage it, so the rag will stop any fluid spreading.

Inspecting drum-brake linings
Every 20 000 km (12 000 miles), the brake linings should be checked for wear and drums for condition.

The removal of the drums is quite simple. Jack up the car and remove road wheels (rear wheels only on 1275GT, as disc brakes are used at the front). Let off the brake adjusters completely at each backplate, then undo the two Phillips (cross-headed) screws that pass through the face of each brake drum to secure it to the wheel-hub flange. The brake drum can then be pulled off the wheel studs, exposing the brake-shoe assemblies.

Check the amount of lining left on each shoe and if it has worn down to about 1·60 mm (0·062 in), a replacement set of shoes will have to be fitted as described later. If the linings are still satisfactory, then simply clean out the brake dust from the drum and brake plate, add a tiny amount of lubricating oil to the adjuster mechanism, then replace the drum. Finally, readjust the brakes in the normal way.

Cleaning vacuum-servo air-filter chamber
This attention is also only required at 20 000-km (12 000-mile) intervals and only applies to the Mini 1275GT cars as they have servo-assisted brakes.

To give easier access to the air-valve cover securing screws, take off the heater air-intake duct as follows: From beneath the wing, pull the intake hose off the duct, and then withdraw the 'push-in' type duct from inside the engine compartment.

After removing the five securing screws, take off the air-valve cover which contains the filter (see Fig. 49). By pushing the air valve off its seat and blowing compressed air at low pressure into it, will clean out the filter of any collected dirt. The cover can then be replaced and the heater air-intake duct refitted.

If the air valve is suspected of not working, or the valve and filter become blocked, then a complete new air-valve assembly should be purchased and fitted.

BLEEDING THE BRAKES
Having dealt with all of the regular maintenance jobs

50. Bleeding the brakes
The bleed valve should be unscrewed one full turn when bleeding the brakes.
There is one bleed valve to each wheel.
The bleed valve for front disc brakes is shown in Fig. 46, item (4).

listed in servicing schedules, it is worthwhile covering a few other items that the keen owner might be faced with. The first of these is brake bleeding. If a new hydraulic pipe is fitted, or any other part of the hydraulic system disturbed, or if the level in the fluid container on the master-cylinder is ever allowed to drop so low that air enters the system, the brakes must be bled to remove any air present.

Fill the reservoir as described previously under 'Routine maintenance' and, commencing at the wheel cylinder nearest the master-cylinder (right-hand front), attach a rubber bleed tube to the bleed valve nipple protruding from the rear of the brake backplate (there is one on each brake)—on front disc brakes of 1275GT cars, the bleed nipple is situated on the top of the back of the brake caliper. Immerse the other end of the tube into a jar containing a little clean fluid and slacken the bleed valve one full turn.

As an assistant slowly pumps down the brake pedal watch the fluid entering the jar. At first air bubbles will be seen and the pedal must continue to be pumped until the fluid that enters the jar does so with no bubbles at all present. When this point is reached, the bleed valve must be tightened as the assistant is pumping the pedal on a *downstroke*. Do not tighten it as the pedal is returning or some air may be drawn back into the system.

Top up the reservoir again and turn to the back-plate next nearest to the master-cylinder (left-hand front) and repeat the procedure, subsequently moving further away from the master-cylinder until all four brakes have been bled—topping up the reservoir between each operation. Do *not* use brake fluid from the jar when topping up as this is aerated; use new fluid. The fluid pumped through the system can be used again, but it must be left standing at least twenty-four hours to allow all the air present in it to escape.

An important point when dealing with the master-cylinder, whether just topping up at services or when bleeding the brakes, is that cleanliness *must* be observed at all times.

RELINING DRUM BRAKES

It has already been explained earlier in this chapter how to remove the brake drums for inspection. When the lining material on the brake shoes wears down to about 1·60 mm (0·062 in), then it is time to fit a set of relined shoes. These can be obtained from any British Leyland dealer on an exchange basis with the dealer taking the old shoes in and giving an allowance against them.

Having proceeded as far as getting the drums off, make a sketch of the positioning of the shoes and return springs to ensure correct replacement. Note that the recessed end of each shoe faces the forward direction of wheel rotation (see Figs. 47 and 48). On

front brakes, first withdraw the spring-loaded hooks (5), Fig. 47 from their registers in the pistons and turn them to one side. Dealing with one backplate at a time, grasp the top shoe and pull it upwards against the tension of the return springs; when it comes clear of the wheel cylinder or abutment pull it away from the backplate and allow it to drop so that the bottom shoe falls away as well.

With the shoes off, thoroughly clean the backplate and wheel cylinder; with the floating wheel cylinder on the rear brakes make sure it slides up and down by lubricating its slide with a little grease. Fit the return springs to the new shoes and locate the bottom shoe in place against the wheel cylinders. Holding it there, pull up the top shoe against the springs until that too can be located against the wheel cylinders.

Once the shoes are in place they can be tapped to one side or another to line them up perfectly ready for the replacement of the brake drum. When fitting of new shoes has been carried out to all the brakes and with all the drums replaced, it is only necessary to adjust the brakes and replace the road wheels to complete the job.

REPLACING A BRAKE HOSE

Should one of the rubber flexible brake hoses split or become porous it is quite a simple matter to replace. The most important thing to remember is to buy the correct hose from a BLMC dealer; do not fit a non-genuine hose as it could be dangerous.

To remove the damaged hose, first unscrew the tube nut (1), Fig. 51. Then, whilst holding the union hexagon (2) to prevent the hose twisting, unscrew locknut (3). Remove the lockwasher and extract the hose from the bracket. Unscrew the other end of the hose from either the wheel cylinder, brake caliper (or the clutch slave cylinder). Plug the exposed port and discard the old copper washer.

When fitting the new hose, use a new copper

51. Removing brake hose
First unscrew tube nut (1), hold hexagon (2) and unscrew locknut (3). Remove lockwasher and extract hose from bracket. The other end of the hose is simply unscrewed off its fitment.

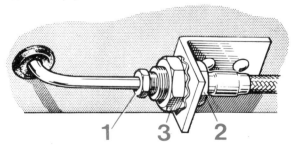

washer and connect the hose to the hydraulic assembly, tightening sufficiently to prevent leakage, but do not overtighten. Next pass the hose union through the mounting bracket, and whilst holding the union (2) with a spanner to prevent the hose from twisting, fit the lockwasher and locknut (3). Ensure the hose is clear of all parts likely to cause chafing.

Reconnect the fluid pipe by screwing in the tube nut (1) sufficiently to prevent fluid leakage; do not overtighten.

Sometimes it may only be a faulty washer which is causing a leak from a pipe or hose union, but remember that whenever the system is disturbed, even to fit a washer, the brakes have to be bled afterwards.

BRAKING FAULTS AND REMEDIES

With the braking system it is easier to list the complaints and the main causes so that quick reference can be made.

1. If the brake pedal needs excessive pressure to stop the car, check:

(a) The shoes are adjusted correctly.

(b) There is no grease or brake fluid on the linings.

(c) The brake drums or discs are not scored or cracked.

(d) The linings or pads are not worn right down.

(e) The handbrake cables are adjusted correctly.

(f) The wheel cylinders are not seized.

2. If the pedal is 'spongy' check:

(a) There is no air in the system; bleed the brakes.

(b) The master-cylinder and wheel-cylinder cups are in order.

3. If the brakes pull to one side check:

(a) There is no grease or brake fluid on the linings.

(b) The drums or discs are not cracked or distorted.

(c) The steering joints are not worn excessively.

(d) The brake backplates are not loose.

(e) The tyre pressures are correct.

(f) The wheel cylinders are not seized.

4. If the brakes come on with a 'snatch' check:

(a) The shoes are correctly adjusted.

(b) The drums or discs are not cracked or distorted.

(c) There is no grease or brake fluid on the linings.

(d) The brake drums or discs are not badly scored.

(e) The brake backplates are not loose.

5. If the brakes 'hang-on' and do not free, check:

(a) The brake shoes are not over-adjusted.

(b) The shoe return springs are not broken or weak.

(c) The handbrake cables are not seized.

(d) The wheel cylinders are not seized.

(e) One of the flexible hoses is not blocked.

Chapter 9

Clutch and transmission

The clutch on all Minis is of rather unorthordox design as it was designed specifically for transverse-engined cars. It transmits the drive downwards via an idler gear to a gearbox/final drive assembly that is fitted where the sump is located on conventional engines. As a result of this, the same lubricating oil accomodates all the units.

CLUTCH

This is of the single-plate dry type with the pressure and driven plates operating on the inner face of the engine flywheel rather than the outer face as is the case with conventional cars. Lugs on the pressure plate pass through the flywheel and are connected to the pressure spring housing by three shouldered bolts. There is a single-plate diaphragm spring located under the cover which pulls the pressure plate rearwards, thus gripping the driven plate between it and the flywheel face providing the required drive to the gearbox input shaft.

The clutch is disengaged by means of a thrust bearing which runs against a thrust plate connected to the clutch cover. As the clutch pedal is depressed it operates a piston in the master cylinder which pressurises the pipeline, causing the clutch slave-cylinder piston to move out, pushing the thrust-bearing operating lever before it. The thrust bearing is forced down onto the thrust plate and when the pressure is applied to the clutch cover, the diaphragm spring takes a flat shape rather than its normal concave shape and the pressure plate is moved away from the driven plate, leaving it free to spin without transmitting any drive.

As the pedal is let off, the pressure on the thrust plate decreases and the diaphragm spring takes over. It slowly returns to its 'free' shape, causing the pressure plate to slowly grip the driven plate and transmit drive to the gearbox.

The advantages of this kind of clutch as compared with the earlier coil-spring type are: less pedal pressure is required to clear the clutch; the take up of drive is more progressive—thus lessening 'kangerooing' away from rest—and the diaphragm spring is more durable than multi-coil springs.

ROUTINE MAINTENANCE
Topping up clutch master cylinder
Every 5 000 km (3 000 miles), check the level of the fluid in the clutch master cylinder. This is situated under the bonnet, attached to the bulkhead next to the brake master cylinder (see Fig. 42). Wipe the top of the reservoir clean as it is vitally important that no dirt or grease enters the system. Remove the filler cap, and using the same fluid that is used in the brake system (UNIPART 410 or 550 brake fluid), top up the reservoir until the level of the fluid is at the bottom of the filler neck. The cap can then be replaced.

Clutch adjustment
At 10 000 km (6 000 mile) periods, the clearance between the clutch-operating lever and its adjustable stop must be checked to ensure the correct clearance is present between the release bearing and the thrust plate inside the clutch housing. It is important that this clearance be kept correct for, as the clutch wears, the clearance diminishes and, if left without attention, the clutch will start to slip.

Pull the operating lever outwards against the pull of the spring until all free movement is taken up and it can be pulled no further. Check with feeler gauges that there is a clearance of 0·5 mm (0·020 in) between the operating lever and the head of the adjustment bolt (see Fig. 52). If the clearance is wrong slacken the locknut and move the adjuster bolt in or out until the correct gap is obtained. Finally, tighten the locknut.

Clutch linkage
The clutch pedal is situated directly beneath the master cylinder and is connected to it by a yoke. From the master to the slave cylinder, the hydraulic pressure is carried by pipes and the only mechanical points are

where the operating lever is attached to the slave cylinder and where the lever enters the clutch housing.

Although it is not in the servicing lists, every 10 000 km (6 000 miles) it is advantageous to add a few drops of oil to these fulcrum points.

Hydraulic lines
There are only two pipes involved in this system; a curved steel pipe which runs from the top of the master cylinder to a bracket on the bulkhead, and from there a moulded rubber hose goes to the slave cylinder. The points to keep under observation are the unions on the top of the master cylinder (where the rubber and steel pipes join), and the point where the rubber pipe enters the slave cylinder.

If a leak is found, it will probably be from one of these points and all that need be done is to disconnect the union nut and fit a new washer. Should a pipe split or become porous it can easily be replaced by disconnecting the unions (see Fig. 51).

CLUTCH FAULTS AND REMEDIES
The main causes of clutch troubles are incorrect adjustment and oil getting on to the linings. The more common clutch faults and their causes and remedies are given below.

Clutch does not clear
This fault becomes apparent when gears cannot be

52. Clutch operating-lever clearance should be checked every 10 000 km (6 000 miles)
Pull back the clutch lever (1) against its spring until all free movement is taken up. The clearance between the operating lever and its stop should be 0·5 mm (0·020 in). Adjust to give the clearance if necessary by slackening the locknut (2) and turning the adjusting screw (3).
Do not forget to tighten the locknut again.

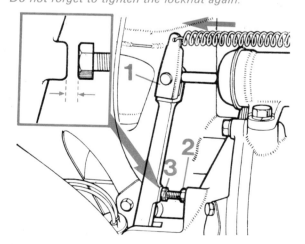

engaged without grinding or using undue force, even though the clutch pedal is fully depressed. In most cases it is due to incorrect adjustment and the lever clearance must be checked as described above. If it is found that this produces no improvement, then it is very likely that the clutch-driven plate has worn down and a new one must be fitted.

It has been known for the clutch pedal to be obstructed by the carpets, especially where thick underfelt is used or rubber mats employed. This, of course, does not allow the pedal to travel as far as it should and gives the same results as incorrect adjustment.

Clutch judder
If, when moving away from rest, a jerky motion of the car takes place and you find it is impossible to make a clean getaway, then the clutch is 'juddering'.

This can be caused by several things; oil on the driven plate, distorted driven plate, engine mountings or tie-bar broken or slack. These must be checked in turn and any faulty points rectified.

Clutch slip
During acceleration, if the engine speed increases without a proportionate increase in the speed of the car it is a sure sign that the clutch is slipping. More often than not it is due to incorrect adjustment or a sticking operating lever at the point it enters the clutch housing, which means that the spring cannot exert its full force.

Excess oil deposits on the driven-plate linings will also cause slip and when a clutch plate is renewed because of this, be sure that the oil leak which allowed oil into the clutch is rectified also.

CLUTCH OVERHAUL
In these days of reconditioned units it is hardly worthwhile a private owner attempting to overhaul a unit. It is much quicker and safer to buy a reconditioned part and simply do a changeover. This idea is certainly the best when dealing with the clutch. Reconditioned master and slave cylinders are available but pressure plate assemblies and driven plates have to be purchased outright.

It is not beyond the scope of a normal motorist to fit the hydraulic units, but it is not advisable to try and fit new driven or pressure-plate parts as special tools are required when setting up the parts and assembling the clutch housing.

Do not forget that if the hydraulic system is disturbed in any way and air is allowed to enter the system it must be bled upon assembly. A bleed-valve nipple is situated on the slave cylinder and the job is carried out in exactly the same way as brake bleeding except there is only one nipple to bleed, and, of course, the clutch pedal is pumped instead of the brake pedal.

TRANSMISSION

The gearbox and differential assemblies are situated together in a common casing which is attached to the underside of the engine in place of a sump. An idler gear transfers the drive from the clutch to the gearbox first-motion shaft and another gear with straight cut teeth on the end of the mainshaft is in constant mesh with the crownwheel. Two short drive-shafts carry the drive from the differential assembly to the front wheels. The outer ends of the shafts are equipped with Birfield constant-velocity universal joints, whilst the inner ends have sliding couplings connected to the drive flanges by small 'U' bolts and rubber bushes.

Operation

The operation of the transmission is rather involved and difficult to describe fully in the space available, but the path of the drive can be traced. When the clutch-driven plate is being gripped and turned by the engine it drives through to a gear train connected to the gearbox input shaft. This, in turn, drives the gearbox layshaft cluster and, depending upon which gear is selected, back through to the mainshaft. The differential 'pinion' on the end of the mainshaft drives the crownwheel at the selected speed ratio and normal differential planet gears transfer the drive to each of the drive shafts. These act as in a normal differential, i.e. as the vehicle corners, the inner driving wheel slows down and the outer one speeds up, whilst the constant-velocity joint give a smooth drive whatever angle the front wheels happen to be, in any plane.

Routine maintenance

As already stated there is no separate lubricant for the gearbox and differential as they share the oil used by the engine and, for this reason, we must impress once again the importance of regular oil and filter changes. The only job to appear on the servicing lists is that every 10 000 km (6 000 miles), the nuts and bolts on the universal joints should be checked for tightness and the power-unit mounting bolts tightened if required.

TRANSMISSION FAULTS AND REMEDIES

Although no work can be carried out on this unit by a private owner, unless he has the special tools needed to dismantle it, it is worthwhile being able to diagnose a fault when one comes to light as he then knows whether or not it is immediately serious.

Noisy transmission

Test with the car moving and also when stationary and out of gear. If the noise is present when moving in one or all ratios, then the gears or bearings are worn. If it is only there when stationary, the fault can lie with either (a) worn constant-mesh gears, (b) worn idler gear or idler-gear bearings, (c) worn first-motion shaft bearing. There are three main types of transmission noise: whine—which is more often due to worn ball races, knocking—which could be chipped or broken gears or balls or a piece of alien material in the box, and roughness—which is nearly always due to excessively worn or pitted races.

Faulty selection

This can be split up into three main subjects;

(a) Auto-disengagement of gear—This can be due to one or more of the following; weak selector springs, worn selector rods and balls, or worn gears.

(b) Stiffness in engagement—Check the gear lever ball-joint for binding, a partly seized relay change lever, faulty synchromesh assembly.

(c) Gears jamming in engagement—This is due to either the synchromesh cones or the selector levers jamming. Before going so far as to dismantle the transmission try an additive (such as Redex or Molyslip) in the oil for a short period as this may free the offending part.

Loss of drive

With the gearbox and differential being together it is impossible to isolate the cause to either one of these units. As the trouble could lie with either of them it is best to list the possible causes of loss of drive.

(a) Mainshaft or first-motion shaft of gearbox fractured.

(b) Constant-mesh gears stripped, either gearbox or differential.

(c) Differential planet-gear pins fractured.

(d) Final-drive flange splines fractured.

(e) Gears on train between clutch and gearbox stripped.

Of course, these are only the faults inside the transmission casing. Loss of drive can also occur— and more often than not does—because of a clutch fault and this should always be the first thing checked. As well as these, the front drive shafts must be looked at, although it is very unlikely, one of them may have sheared or a universal-joint flange broken.

AUTOMATIC TRANSMISSION

As an alternative, Mini models can be purchased with the fully automatic four-speed transmission designed for BLMC by Automotive Products; this is designed to allow the driver to select any of the gears manually and hold them if he wishes to override the automatic selection at any time. In this respect it offers the best of both worlds; automatic changing when driving might be tiring in congested streets, or manual changing when full performance potential might be wanted on the open road.

Drive to the transmission is via a torque converter

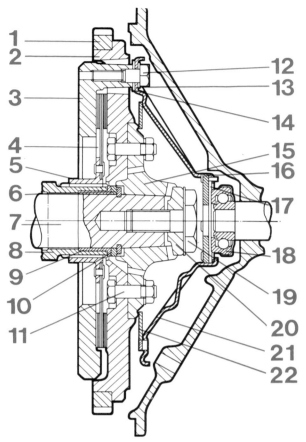

53. Section through diaphragm-spring clutch assembly

1. Starter ring
2. Flywheel
3. Pressure plate
4. Driven plate
5. Driven-plate hub
6. Circlip
7. Crankshaft
8. Crankshaft primary gear
9. Primary gear bearing
10. Thrust washer
11. Flywheel-hub bolt
12. Driving pin
13. Lock washer
14. Driving strap
15. Flywheel hub
16. Thrust plate
17. Plate-retaining spring
18. Thrust bearing
19. Flywheel screw
20. Keyed washer
21. Cover
22. Diaphragm spring

however, therefore it is possible to notice a small fall-off in performance with the automatic model due to the slight power loss through the converter. The torque converter takes the place of the clutch on normal models, it being a three-element unit with a maximum conversion ratio of 2:1.

When the torque converter is transmitting drive to the gearbox it is via an idler gear to the input shaft, the gearbox itself having a bevel gear train providing four forward and one reverse gear. Selection of the gears is by application of brake bands for reverse, second and third, while top is direct drive through a multi-disc clutch with the gear train locked up.

Operation

A selector lever is mounted in the front floor of the car between the seats, this having seven positions, R, N. D, 1, 2, 3, 4. Reverse can be selected by lifting the lever over an abutment on the quadrant. With the lever in *D,* the car will move off by application of the throttle to increase engine speed, changing gear automatically as predetermined road speeds are reached in each gear. For better acceleration and delaying changing up, as one would want for over-taking, there is a 'kick-down' switch under the throttle pedal. When the throttle is opened and held right down, the car will hold on to each gear for a much longer period before changing up, unless the throttle pedal is let off, in which case the box will immediately change up if the car is running above the speed for the gear which it happens to be in at the time.

When the driver wishes to change gear manually he simply shifts the lever through the 1, 2, 3 and 4 positions in turn, holding each gear for as long as he wishes. The valve block which applies the hydraulic pressures for the brake bands and multi-disc clutch is then being operated manually, therefore the box will not change gear until the lever is moved. The second, third and top gears all provide engine braking when on the overrun, whether the operation is automatic or manual, therefore the driver must be careful not to change down manually at too high a road speed otherwise serious damage to the trans-mission might result.

Servicing

The oils listed in Chapter 3 for the power unit also apply for automatic models—the oil-change period is every 10 000 km (6 000 miles)—the only differ-ence being in the method of checking the oil level after replacement of the oil in the power unit.

With the automatic models, the power-unit oil is drained in the same way by removing the magnetic drain plug, then refilled by the orifice in the rocker cover. To check the level however, the engine must be run for two minutes, switched off, then the dip-stick withdrawn straight away to see the level. Fill with oil until the correct level is reached by this method.

As far as the private owner is concerned, nothing else can be done to the automatic transmission. A complete range of special tools and hydraulic pres-sure-testing equipment is needed before any work or diagnosis can be carried out. The transmission needs no other servicing and has proved to be extremely reliable.

Chapter 10

Steering, wheels and tyres

With this rack-and-pinion steering gear, the rack housing is attached to the bulkhead behind the power unit. The rack itself, which is a piece of steel rod, has teeth machined along part of its length on one side and runs through the middle of the rack housing. The teeth are hardened against wear.

Engaging with the teeth on the rack is a pinion gear which is supported in the rack housing by means of ball bearings. The pinion shaft is sealed against oil leakage from the rack housing and is splined so that it mates with the lower end of the steering column, this being secured by a pinch-bolt.

A spring-loaded damper pad enters the underside of the rack housing and bears against the rack thereby taking up any excess play between the teeth by keeping them firmly together. This damper consists of a separate housing, a pad and a spring. Shims are interposed between the damper housing and rack housing, thus allowing adjustment to be made to the tension of the spring.

At each outer end of the rack a ball-joint connects a tie-rod with an adjustable end to the steering arms on the front hubs. Rubber gaiters are used at these points to ensure that no lubricant is lost from the rack housing.

WHEELS AND TYRES

The Clubman and Estate are both fitted with 3·50B–10 pressed-steel wheels and 5·20–10 cross-ply tyres as standard, although it is possible to order the car ex-works with radial-ply tyres fitted as an optional extra. The 1275GT is fitted with 4·50J–10 Rostyle wheels and 145–10 radial tyres, as standard.

All wheels have four-stud fixing to the hubs and the wheel nuts are countersunk to locate with the wheels, so ensure they are always fitted the right way round.

ROUTINE MAINTENANCE

At weekly intervals, the wheel discs should be removed so that the wheel nuts can be checked for tightness. If the owner has a torque wrench it is advisable to keep the nuts at their recommended setting of 5·8 kg-m (42 lb-ft). Once the nuts have been checked, inspect tyre pressures. Those below the set figures must be inflated to bring them up to the factory recommended pressures of:

Cross-ply tyres—front 1·7 kg/cm² (24 lb/in²);
rear 1·5 kg/cm² (22 lb/in²).
When fully loaded it is permissible to have both front and rear tyres at 1·7 kg/cm² (24 lb/in²).
Radial-ply tyres (all conditions) —
front 2·0 kg/cm² (28 lb/in²);
rear 1·8 kg/cm² (26 lb/in²).

Front-wheel alignment

There are certain critical angles in the design of the steering system and front suspension which affect steering and riding qualities, road holding and tyre wear. The kingpin (swivel-hub) inclination, camber angle and castor angle need not concern the owner, though they should be checked by a dealer if ever the car is involved in a severe collision.

The front-wheel alignment, however, should be checked every 10 000 km (6 000 miles). The toe-out of the front wheels should be 1·6 mm (0·062 in), that is, the distance between the high points of the tyre walls measured on the centre line of the wheels at the rear should be 1·6 mm less than the measurement taken at the corresponding point at the front of the wheels, with the wheels in the straight-ahead position.

The steering tie-rods are provided with screwed adjusters which allow the correct toe-out to be obtained, but adjustment should be left to a dealer who has available an optical alignment gauge.

The usual signs of faulty alignment are rapid wear on the front tyres, with fins of rubber appearing along one edge of each groove in the treads.

Lubrication of swivel-hub ball-joints

There are two greasing points each side on the

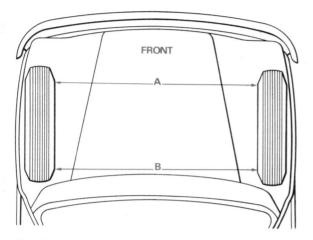

54. Front-wheel alignment
The wheel alignment on Mini models is set in a 'toe-out' position rather than a 'toe-in'.
The measurement A should be 1·6 mm (0·062 in) longer than B.

steering that need attention with a grease gun every 5 000 km (3 000 miles). There is one at the top of each swivel hub and another at the bottom of each hub (see Fig. 55).

To ensure full penetration of the lubricant, it is advisable to first jack up the car. If the nipples are already filled with grease no further lubricant can usually be forced in.

Steering-rack lubrication

The steering rack needs no routine attention as it is filled with oil when it is assembled and need only be refilled during an overhaul. As this is the case, there are no oiling nipples and if a leak occurs at any time (perhaps from one of the rubber gaiters) the following procedure must be adopted:

Jack up the front of the car and place it on stands. Remove the retaining clip and release the rubber gaiter from the right-hand end of the rack housing. Turn the steering until the wheels are in the straight-ahead position and insert an oil nozzle into the end of the rack housing. Pump in not more than 0·18 litre (0·33 UK pint) of SAE 90 Hypoid oil of one of the recommended makes. Reconnect the rubber gaiter and tighten its clip, finally moving the steering *slowly* from lock to lock so that the oil is distributed evenly throughout the housing. It is dangerous to swing the steering quickly from one lock to the other, especially after having refilled the housing, as the oil may collect in one end and burst the rubber gaiter.

STEERING CONNECTIONS

Rack-and-pinion steering has very few joints and

mountings. U-bolts secure the rack housing to the car body bulkhead, a clamp bolt secures the column to the pinion, and two ball-joints connect the tie-rods to the front-hub steering arms.

All of these steering nuts and bolts should have their tightness checked every 5 000 km (3 000 miles) to ensure none are working loose.

Checking for wear

As the mileage of the car increases it will be found that the tie-rod ends will wear, leading to various steering complaints. To check the ends for wear, the car should be jacked up and stands placed underneath. Lying under the car grasp one end of the tie-rod near the joint and work it up and down. If it is badly worn, the ball-cup cover, which fits snugly against the hole in the steering arm, will move away from the arm and, in fact, the joint will be felt to be

55. Grease nipples each side of the steering
Nipples (1) and (2) are for lubricating the top and bottom ball-joints upon which the front-wheel hub swivels.
The steering tie-rod ball-joint (3) is sealed during manufacture and requires no further lubrication.

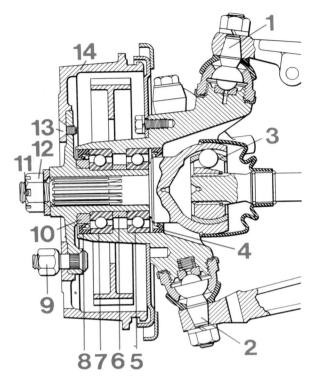

56. The front hub assembly—Clubman models

Taper-roller bearings are used on 1275GT cars.
1. *Hub-swivel ball-joint (top)*
2. *Hub-swivel ball-joint (bottom)*
3. *Constant-velocity universal joint*
4. *Inner oil-seal*
5. *Inner ball bearing*
6. *Bearing inner spacer*
7. *Outer ball bearing*
8. *Outer oil-seal*
9. *Wheel nut (4 off)*
10. *Bearing outer spacer*
11. *Split-pin*
12. *Hub nut*
13. *Brake-drum securing screw (2 off)*
14. *Brake drum*

slack. When this point is reached, it is vital that the joints be renewed as quickly as possible as when they are worn, the shear stress on them is much greater and they *could* fracture, causing a serious accident.

There are no swivel pins on the steering of these cars, instead the front hubs have ball-joints at the top and bottom, these joints being anchored on the outer ends of the suspension wishbone arms. The steering therefore swivels on ball-joints and not on

pins. The lubrication of these joints has been described earlier and they are designed and made from the best materials to give long and satisfactory service, providing they are lubricated regularly. When the joints do eventually wear, they can be checked by jacking up the front end of the car and taking hold of the wheel at the top and bottom and moving it in and out in a vertical plane. Whilst doing this an assistant can watch the top and bottom ball-joints and the amount of wear can be seen.

FRONT HUBS

Two ball-bearing races (taper-roller bearings on 1275GT) are used in each front hub and they are packed with grease during assembly and need no further attention until they are dismantled for overhaul. Two oil-seals in each hub are used to keep in the grease and, whilst the outer one on each side is quite easy to replace, the inner one involves the removal of the drive-shafts and is best left to a dealer as special tools are required.

When the hub bearings wear excessively, there will be no need for checking as they will give plenty of warning. At first, when the wear is slight, a low 'moan' will be heard when running in any gear; as the wear gets worse so will the noise, until it reaches a high-pitched whine. The bearings should be renewed at the first sign of wear to lessen the chance of the other steering parts becoming worn.

STEERING FAULTS

The most common causes of steering troubles are wear in the components (especially after a considerable mileage has been covered), worn tyres or incorrect wheel balance. A number of steering faults are given below.

Excessive free play at steering wheel—The most probable cause of this complaint is wear between the rack-and-pinion or worn ball-joints on the tie-rod ends. To rectify the former, the rack must be adjusted by means of its damper to bring the teeth into closer mesh; with the latter new ends are needed on the tie-rods as they are not adjustable.

Wheel wobble—This may be due to unbalanced wheels and tyres (see later), worn wheel bearings, wear in the steering unit or ball-joints, damage through collision to the front suspension, or incorrect steering angles (see under 'Front-wheel alignment' above).

Car tends to wander—This can be caused by incorrect tyre pressures, very uneven tyre wear, wear in the steering unit or ball-joints, incorrect steering angles, weak shock absorbers, or misalignment of the front suspension.

Steering feels 'heavy'—Caused by incorrect steering angles (see above), very low tyre pressures, too tightly adjusted steering-rack damper, lack of lubrication in the steering unit or joints, or faulty front-wheel alignment.

Tyre squeal—Caused usually by very low tyre pressures or incorrect steering angles.

The remedies for all these faults are self-evident. It should also be noted that faulty steering, for any reason, almost always results in rapid wear on the front tyres, and for this reason as well as considerations of safety should never be neglected.

TYRE LIFE

Having already covered the routine maintenance of the tyres, it is also worthwhile mentioning some other small points which should regularly be seen to. As well as the wheel changes and pressure checks, to obtain maximum tyre life carry out the following jobs from time to time.

Keep the treads free from stones and grit and carry out any necessary repairs. Clean the wheel rims and keep them free from rust, paint them if required.

Should the tyres get oily use petrol, sparingly, to wipe off the oil and dry them thoroughly afterwards.

Avoid under- or over-inflation at all costs.

Keep the clutch and brakes correctly adjusted and in good order, if they become 'fierce' or uneven in their action it has very destructive effects upon the tyres.

Do not 'kerb' the tyres at any time and take care not to allow them to suffer severe impact.

Note—It is an offence if a tyre does not have a tread pattern at least 1 mm deep in a continuous band of pattern at least three-quarters of the tread width. It is also an offence if the tyre is unsuitable either in itself or in combination with other tyres on the vehicle; not properly inflated; or has a break in its fabric or a serious cut, a lump or bulge caused by ply separation or failure, or any portion of the ply structure exposed.

TUBELESS TYRE REPAIRS

Simple punctures in tubeless tyres caused by nails, etc., can usually be temporarily repaired without removing the wheel from the car by using an appropriate tubeless tyre-repair kit.

It is the opinion of the tyre manufacturers that a single plug repair is merely a temporary expedient which the motorist himself can carry out provided he follows precisely the instructions on the repair kit; such a repair must be made permanent by the addition of a cold patch or a properly vulcanised repair as soon as possible afterwards.

Where tubeless tyres have been completely deflated, it is essential to have a supply of compressed air to re-inflate them and this job should be carried out by a garage.

TYRE VALVES

As tubeless tyres are employed, a mushroom-headed rubber valve is used. It is secured in the wheel by a small stepped flange on the valve itself and also by the pressure of the air inside the tyre.

To test a valve for air-tightness, rotate the wheel until the valve is at the top and then inserting its end into a small container of water (an egg-cup is useful for this). If bubbles appear, the valve seating is faulty and the core must be replaced by using a pair of pin-nosed pliers to unscrew it from the valve body. Whether faulty or not it is advisable to renew the valve cores every twelve months. Valve caps, as well as keeping out undesirable elements such as grit and dirt, also act as secondary air seals and should therefore always be fitted.

WHEEL BALANCING

When a wheel is out of balance, it has a heavy point which makes it always come to rest in the same position after rotating freely. The heavy point is more often to be found on the tyre than the wheel itself. This lack of balance can reduce riding comfort, affect steering at fast speeds, and produce irregular tyre wear.

A British Leyland dealer has special equipment with which wheels can be balanced both statically and dynamically, and can quickly carry out this job whenever new tyres are fitted. This is important in the case of the front wheels, less so in the case of the rear wheels since these do not affect steering.

Chapter 11

Front and rear suspension

When the Minis were first announced in 1959 they were fitted with a revolutionary suspension system which other than the positioning of the engine, was the most widely hailed breakthrough. For the first time on a production car rubber spring units were used instead of coil, leaf or torsion-bar metal springing. This method was later developed to incorporate a fluid so that there were two suspension mediums—rubber under compression and fluid under high pressure. The new system was designated Hydrolastic and eventually came to be used on other, larger, British Leyland cars.

Although the Mini Clubman and 1275GT models were not introduced until October 1969, it transpires that both of the above types of suspension have been used. On their introduction, the saloon cars were fitted with Hydrolastic suspension and the estate model with the original rubber spring set-up; this was critised by both the motoring press and the public, mainly because of the bouncy ride that Hydrolastic gave on such small saloons and British Leyland decided to revert to the rubber spring unit suspension on all models.

Owners will find that from the following Commission Numbers, the cars have rubber springing, and prior to these numbers on Clubman Saloon and 1275GT, Hydrolastic suspension is fitted:

Clubman Saloon:

Commission No. S20S 48645A (manual models)
Commission No. S20S 48268A (automatics)

1275GT:

Commission No. S20D 8156A

The original rubber-cone spring suspension system will be dealt with first, as in fact the arrangement of the suspension arms and struts is the same for both systems.

ARRANGEMENT OF FRONT SUSPENSION

The front suspension consists of upper and lower wishbones connected at their outer ends to the swivel hubs by means of ball-joints. The inner ends pivot about pins passing through lugs on the side members of the front sub-frame. Towards the inner end of the top wishbone, a socket is provided for the ball end of a short trumpet-shaped strut, the top of this strut fitting into the metal insert of the spring unit. The other side of the spring unit fits snugly against a special housing which is part of the sub-frame.

From this, it can be seen that as a wheel rides over an obstruction the wishbones move up about their pivots; this movement being felt by the strut which tries to move the spring unit. However, as this is secured at its top, the rubber cone flexes thereby giving the wheel the necessary movement. The suspension of each front wheel is quite independent of the other.

57. Sectioned view of the rubber-cone spring unit and its strut inside the front sub-frame tower

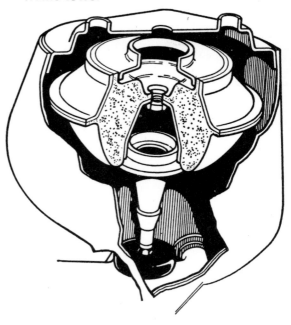

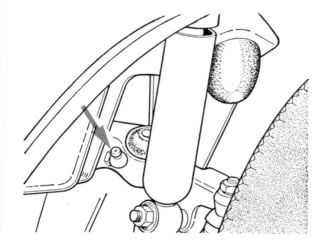

58. Front-suspension lubrication—rubber-cone spring suspension

The grease nipple which lubricates the upper support-arm inner pivot. A similar nipple is situated on the other front side of the car.

ARRANGEMENT OF REAR SUSPENSION

At the rear, the suspension is similar to that above—if it could be imagined turned through 90°. The wheel hubs are attached to large trailing arms which pivot about pins through the rear sub-frame.

On the underside of these arms are sockets which hold the ball end of rather long trumpet-shaped struts, the other end of the struts fitting into the metal insert in the bottom of the spring unit. Again the other side of the spring unit fits against a special housing in the sub-frame. As the wheel is deflected the strut is pushed into the rubber cone, which deflects because its other side is hard against the frame.

SHOCK ABSORBERS (DAMPERS)

Both front and rear rubber-cone suspensions use tubular telescopic shock absorbers, these being interposed between the top wishbone and the wing valance at the front, and between the trailing arms and special brackets welded to the wheel arches at the rear. Dampers cannot be adjusted or topped up with fluid and when they become defective they must be replaced with reconditioned units.

ROUTINE MAINTENANCE
Lubrication points

There are four grease nipples that require three or four strokes of the grease gun every 5 000 km (3 000 miles). At the front there is a nipple each side on the upper support arm, near the cup which supports the ball end of the suspension strut. At the rear one nipple is provided on each side at the end of the

trailing-arm pivot pin. With the latter, it is important to carry on pumping even after the grease commences to extrude from around the outside edge of the pin; if this is not done the inner bush which carries the pin is starved of lubricant and in time seizes and plays strange tricks on the steering and riding of the car. These greasing points are shown in Figs. 58 and 59.

Checking shock absorbers

Every 5 000 km (3 000 miles) an inspection of all four shock absorbers should be carried out to see if they are leaking. Should a faulty one be found it can be replaced as described later.

At intervals of 10 000 km, the same inspection can be carried out again, but at the same time the top and bottom mounting nuts on the units must be checked and tightened if necessary. The top mounting nuts for the rear shock absorbers can be seen in the luggage boot of saloon models and in the rear of the body with Clubman Estate models. In all cases, the top shock-absorber bolt protrudes through the wheel arch and the nuts are on top covered with a small rubber cup so that things carried in the rear are not 'snagged' at any time.

Fuel tank removal—In the case of saloons, to gain access to the top mounting of the left-hand damper, the petrol tank has to be removed. This entails draining off the petrol by turning the drain plug with a box spanner, aiming the drain tube into a suitable receptacle. With all the fuel out, take the drain plug and tube right off and do not refit them to the tank until it has been put back in the car again at the end of the job.

59. Rear-suspension lubrication—rubber-cone spring suspension

This is the grease nipple for the rear trailing-arm pivot pin; there is one nipple each side of the car.

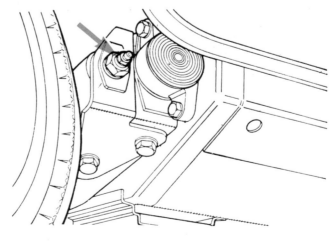

Disconnect the flexible fuel pipe from the fuel pump and remove the tank filler cap, then disconnect the lead attached to the tank gauge unit. Undo the tank securing strap, release the clip retaining the vent pipe, and manoeuvre the tank out of the luggage boot.

Reassembly is the opposite to this, making sure the vent pipe is pushed back through the same hole as the wiring harness and the locating plate is fitted beneath the tank before the securing strap is tightened.

Checking suspension

Also during the 10 000-km (6 000-mile) service, all the suspension nuts and bolts must be checked for tightness and those that require it pulled down until tight. If squeaks become apparent from the suspension, it is very likely that the rubber bushes on the shock absorbers are the cause as they sometimes become dry. To overcome this give all the bushes a liberal application of brake fluid with a paint brush. Do *not* use oil or paraffin on them as these fluids will soon rot the rubber.

REAR HUBS

The rear hubs are secured to the stub axle on each trailing arm by means of a split-pinned nut. There are two bearings in each hub and behind the inner bearing is an oil-seal that stops any grease reaching the brake-shoe linings.

It is quite a simple matter to remove the hub assembly. First remove the wheel and brake drum as described in Chapter 8. Then prise off the hub cap, remove the split-pinned nut from the stub shaft and withdraw the hub assembly.

With the hub off, the seal can be prised from the back and, if necessary, the bearings drifted out with their spacer.

When replacing the bearings, they should be packed with one of the recommended greases and the spacer in between also lightly greased. The hub can be refitted to the stub axle after the oil-seal has been fitted and then any surplus grease wiped away. After the nut has been tightened and split-pinned, the cap can be tapped back into place. On no account should this cap be filled with grease, it should be absolutely dry and clean. The flat washer under the hub-securing nut should be fitted with its chamfered edge towards the outer bearing.

There should be no need to grease the bearings at all during services. The only time grease need be added to the hubs is when they are taken off the car either to fit a new seal or bearings.

SHOCK ABSORBER REPLACEMENT

Both front and rear shock absorbers can be removed fairly easily from their mountings. The method of removal differs for front and rear shock absorbers. Both methods are described below.

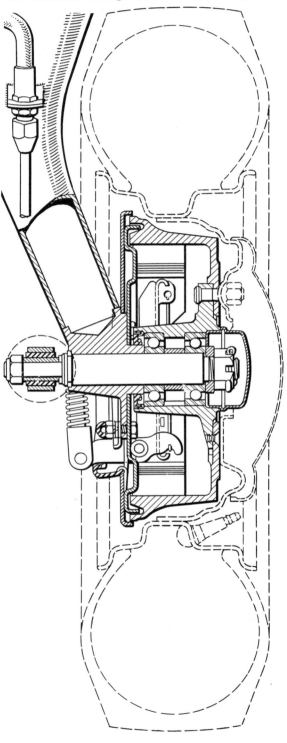

60. Section through rear-hub assembly

Front shock absorbers

Jack up the front of the car and remove the road wheel from the side to be worked upon. Place a support beneath the lower suspension arm, remove the top and bottom mounting nuts and pull the shock absorber from its pins.

Push the rubber bushes from the eyes in the unit and examine them for wear; if they show signs of deterioration buy new ones when purchasing the replacement units. Fit the bushes to the new shock absorber and, holding the bottom end of the unit in a vice, fully extend and compress it about six times to expel any air from the pressure chamber. Keep the shock absorber in an upright position after doing this and fit it to the car exactly opposite to the way it was removed, fully tightening the securing nuts.

Rear shock absorbers

Remove the upper damper securing nuts from inside the car (taking out the petrol tank as described earlier when dealing with the left-hand one on saloon models). Jack up the rear of the car and remove the road wheel, undoing the bottom mounting nut and removing its washer from the unit. Push the damper down until it is fully compressed and remove it from its anchoring pin on the trailing arm of the suspension.

Again push out the bushes and examine them for wear, renewing as required. Hold the new damper in a vice by its bottom eye and extend and compress it several times to expel any air as was done with the front units. Keep it in an upright position after doing this and fit it to the car in the reverse procedure to removal. When raising the trailing arm so that the top of the shock absorber passes through the hole in the wheel arch, make sure that the cone spring unit and the spring strut trumpet are located in their respective pivots. If all is well here, the top mounting rubbers and securing nuts can be fitted and tightened. Failure to observe this instruction could result in the car having a lopsided appearance as the rubber spring or the strut may not be right home; if the vehicle is run in this condition both of these units would very soon be damaged beyond repair.

The above instructions also apply when new shock-absorber bushes are fitted. Whilst on the subject of these bushes, it is advisable to immerse new ones in brake fluid before fitting them to the shock absorbers as they are then well lubricated and are less likely to become noisy.

DISMANTLING THE SUSPENSION

Apart from the servicing covered in this chapter, there are no other jobs that can be carried out by the owner on the suspension as special tools are needed for dismantling. It is not advisable for owners to try and dismantle the suspension at the front without these tools because the rubber spring cones are fitted at a very high rate of compression. If the top wishbone pivot is disturbed without first compressing the spring with a special tool, the strut is likely to jump out of place at a high velocity. It could cause serious damage to anyone in the near vicinity.

HYDROLASTIC SUSPENSION

The mounting of the suspension arms and struts, both front and rear, is the same as for rubber-suspensioned cars, the differences being in the type of bearing material used for the suspension-arm pivots. There is no grease nipple in the upper front-suspension arms, nor on the rear trailing-arm pivot, as these points are lubricated with special molybdenum disulphide grease during assembly and require no further attention until they are dismantled again. There is also no need for shock absorbers on the Hydrolastic system.

At the outer end of the top wishbone is a flat seating, which if the suspension is overworked, comes into contact with the rubber bump block situated directly above it. There is a bump block on the rubber-cone suspension, but with Hydrolastic models, if anything should happen to cause the suspension to drop, the car will only settle on to the bump block and it can be driven safely at speeds up to 50 km/h (30 mile/h) like this on good roads until a repair can be effected.

Suspension fluid

The fluid used in the Hydrolastic system is a mixture of water and alcohol to overcome any freezing tendencies, and an anti-corrosive additive. The fluid system pressure of $20 \cdot 6$ kg/cm² (292 lb/in²) varies slightly to achieve the correct suspension trim setting. There are $2 \cdot 27$ litres (4 UK pints) of fluid in the system which can only be introduced, or the pressures changed, by using a special service tool. Owners must on no account tamper with the Hydrolastic valves situated in the pipes coming from each Hydrolastic suspension unit at the front.

With the car standing on level ground and unladen except for fuel, water and oil, the suspension height can be checked by taking four simple measurements. Remove the wheel discs and take a vertical measurement from the centre of the wheel hub to the bottom edge of the body wing above it.

These measurements, front and rear, should all be 343 mm, plus or minus $9 \cdot 5$ mm ($13 \cdot 5$ in, plus or minus $0 \cdot 375$ in) and if any measurement is found to be incorrect, have the Hydrolastic system fluid pressure adjusted accordingly on that side of the car.

Chapter 12

Bodywork upkeep

The two-door bodywork of the Clubman and 1275GT is of unitary steel construction with the body shell itself being used as a stress-bearing member. The body is specially strengthened to accept the two sub-frame half chassis to which all of the mechanical components are attached. These models differ from the normal range of Minis in appearance due to the squarer front-end treatment with headlamps recessed in the front grille panel and a wider bonnet giving better engine accessibility.

Because of the revised front end, overall length of these models is approximately 127 mm (5 in) more than the standard Minis and Mini-Coopers. The doors have concealed hinges and wind-up windows, no separate quarter-lights being necessary due to the ventilation ducts of the facia. The 1275GT has identification trim lines running along the lower edge of the body on each side.

On saloon models, the boot lid hinges downwards and is supported by two wires so that luggage can be mounted on it if required, and because of this the number plate is hinged along its top edge so that it will hang down when the luggage boot lid is in the open position. Estate cars have two opening rear doors. The luggage boot floor has a soft cover over the spare wheel and battery on Clubman models and a stiff floor panel on the 1275GT.

Front wrap-around bumpers are set quite high, with the number plate and side/flasher lights situated below. Chrome 'underriders' are positioned on the front bumper flanking the number plate.

The interior fittings and instruments are covered in Chapter 1.

SEAT BELTS

A law was passed, such, that all cars registered after 1st January 1965, be fitted with seat belts, and it is strongly recommended that these are always worn. Methods of adjustment vary, but belts should always be worn so that the buckle is positioned at the side of the body by the hip, and not in front of the abdomen. The belts when on should be tight enough to allow a hand to be slipped between the chest and belt webbing; with the automatic reel-type belts this does not apply as they take up their own position and rest lightly against the body at all times.

Seat belt anchorages

There are special built-in points located in the body for mounting the seat belts and these positions are

61. Door interior details
1. Door release lever
2. Window regulator handle
3. Locking latch—move latch rearwards to lock the door, forwards to unlock

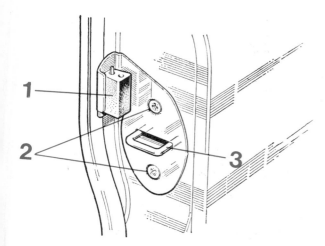

62. Door catch adjustment
1. *Rubber bump stop*
2. *Striker-plate securing screws*
3. *Lock catch (striker) loop*

drilled and stiffened during manufacture. If ever the seat belts are removed from the car at any time they must always be replaced at the correct anchorage points.

The anchorage points are located on the floor tunnel just behind the front seats, on the centre door pillars each side of the car, and inside the door sills. The complete seat-belt assembly that is attached to these points is to a British Standard that ensures it withstands loop loads of over 2 722 kg (6 000 lb).

One final point to remember with seat belts is that if the car has been involved in an accident and the belts have taken an impact strain, then they should be tested by the manufacturers before being used again. Normally, once a strain like this has been put on the webbing new belts are required.

PREVENTING RUST

With this type of body shell it is very important that rust is not allowed to gain a foothold as it will prove to be very costly to repair. Regular inspection should therefore be made to both the underside and topside of the bodywork so that if any signs of deterioration are found, steps can immediately be taken to clean it off.

Regular maintenance should include a weekly wash to remove all traces of mud, as this holds moisture and accelerates the formation of rust; a fortnightly or monthly wax polish as this gives a lasting protection to the paintwork; a regular inspection of the underbody during which the mud and other collected dirt must be washed from the undersides of the wings and body with a hose.

WASHING THE CAR

A soft sponge should be used with plenty of water containing a little mild detergent. If mud deposits are very thick on the paintwork, they must be softened by soaking them well with water before being wiped away, otherwise the paint finish may become scratched. When all traces of mud and dirt are removed a final rinse can be given with plain fresh water and a damp chamois leather used to dry off the paintwork.

If, after washing, there are grease or tar marks present on the paint, use methylated spirits only for their removal and not petrol or paraffin. Finally, touch-in any chips or scratches in the paintwork with the correct colour paint to ensure that rust is not allowed to develop. A dealer will advise if there is any doubt as to the correct colour of the paint.

If the underbody is to be hosed down, it is as well to jack up one side of the vehicle at a time so that the jet of water can be directed well up into the wheel arch and all traces of mud washed away. Any rusty patches on the underside which come to light should be thoroughly cleaned with a wire brush and treated with an anti-corrosive mixture such as Jenolite, before being given a coating of chassis-black.

Where the vehicle has been undersealed, after washing the mud from underneath, the sealing compound should be inspected to see that none has come away. If a bare patch is discovered obtain a little of the compound from a dealer so that it can be brushed on.

POLISHING THE CAR

A good grade of silicone or wax-based polish can be used and it should be applied to the paintwork with a soft, dry cloth. However, a hard wax polish gives a much more lasting protection, but is of course harder and more tiring to apply. If a hard wax polish *is* used, the job should be carried out in the shade or on a cool day, for if it is applied in the direct rays of the sun it will dry so quickly that it will be extremely hard to remove.

A very small portion of the body should be done at a time (for example a wing or quarter of the roof panel) and the wax applied with a piece of dampened mutton cloth. After application, the wax should be polished immediately using plenty of 'elbow grease'.

The beauty of a waxed body is that full protection is given against water and dust and when the body becomes grimy all that need be done is to wipe it over lightly with a damp chamois leather. Naturally, the wax can be used on the interior painted portions of the car with the same good results.

It is important whenever polishing a vehicle that no portion of the polish being used is allowed to reach the windscreen, because as soon as it rains and the wipers are set in motion a smeary film will appear and it will be almost impossible to see through it.

The bright parts of the car, stainless steel and chromium, must not be cleaned with metal polish under any circumstances. They should be washed frequently with soap and water and, when all the dirt has been removed, wiped dry with a damp chamois leather until bright.

Any surface deposits on the chromium-plated parts can be removed with a good grade of chromium cleaner. In the same way, any slight tarnishing of the stainless steel can be removed with impregnated wadding as used to clean household silverware. For protection of the chromium plating, a good coat of hard wax polish every time the car itself is polished will suffice, but during winter months, if real protection is required a chromium protective lacquer can be brushed on.

CLEANING THE INTERIOR

The carpets should be removed prior to polishing and either beaten or vacuumed to remove all the collected dust and dirt. The upholstery, that is the seats and door trim panels, should be cleaned periodically by wiping them over with a damp cloth. If dirt is allowed to accumulate too long it will work its way into the grain of the leathercloth portions and, as well as giving a bad appearance, will also be very hard to remove.

If the surface does become really soiled, warm water and a non-caustic soap should be used with a piece of mutton cloth. The upholstery must not be soaked with water; the mutton cloth only being dampened with the soapy water before being applied. It is vitally important that no detergents, caustic soaps, petrol or any other kinds of spirits are used on the upholstery finish.

LUBRICATION OF BODY PARTS

To get maximum life from door and boot-lid locks, it is important that they should be lightly lubricated with a smear of engine oil every 5 000 km (3 000 miles). At the same time an oilcan should be used to lubricate the door and boot hinges (rear door hinges on the Estate); engine oil can again be used for this operation.

Oil the swivel pin on the bonnet safety catch and apply a little grease to the nose of the actual lock peg and also to the well into which it fits. No other attention is necessary.

DOOR CATCH ADJUSTMENT

The push-button door locks are preset during assembly and should need no attention to their internals, unless at some stage the lock jams completely, in which case the assembly will have to be taken from the doors for repair or replacement.

However, it is sometimes necessary to adjust the door-lock striker plate that is attached to the body door aperture in order to position the door flush with the side of the body. To do this, first slacken the two Phillips (cross-headed) screws (2), Fig. 62, that hold the striker plate to the door aperture, but leave them tight enough to allow the door to shut and move the striker.

Depress the door-lock push-button and pull the latch disc in the lock back to the 'open' position with a screwdriver. Shut the door and allow it to latch, then using the door handle, but not touching the button, pull the door out (or push it in, whichever is relevant) until the door fits flush with the rest of the body.

Use the push-button to open the door and mark with a pencil, the position of the striker plate. Remove the bump rubber stop (1) from the striker plate and while the screws are still slack, set the door-lock catch loop (3) so that it is exactly at right angles to the door aperture. Finally tighten the striker-plate screws, replace the bump rubber stop, and check that when the door is fully shut it is still flush with the body.

The door should shut without any 'lift' or 'drop' as it closes, if there is any sign of either, the striker-plate screws must be slackened again, and keeping the plate within the marks made for its horizontal position, it can be moved up or down until the position is found where the door enters its aperture in the body without any up or down movement.

BODYWORK REPAIRS

If any accidental damage is sustained to the body of the car, a British Leyland dealer is definitely the best person to carry out repairs as they will have the necessary jigs to check the body alignment both before and after the repair to ensure that all the mechanical components attached to the body frames are correctly lined-up. If this is not done, many strange occurrences may come to light, especially with the steering and front suspension, which will prove to be very expensive.

A defective frame may be the cause of the tyres wearing out in a short space of time, or of excess strain being thrown upon the front suspension and steering components, creating excess wear and making the vehicle dangerous to drive. Remember, people trained by the manufacturers—as most Distributor personnel are—must know more about the cars than non-dealers, and they are best equipped to help you if any major mishap occurs.

Chapter 13

Electrical system

A 12-volt negative-earth system is employed on Mini Clubman and 1275GT models, although prior to their introduction in October 1969 all Minis had positive-earth systems. If ever any electrical accessories are purchased make sure at the outset that they are for negative-earth cars, even though the packaging may indicate that the accessory is for a Mini.

The battery is located in the luggage boot under the flooring (under the rear-seat cushion of Estate cars) and when the engine is running, the system incorporates compensated voltage control charging from a dynamo driven by the engine fan belt. It is possible to specify an alternator as optional equipment in place of the dynamo; for cold-country export models this is a standard fitting.

A dynamo is normally a fairly low output direct-current generator, whereas an alternator is an alternating-current generator which provides a high charging rate at relatively low engine speeds and also has a much higher overall output than a dynamo.

Whichever is fitted, both units are made by Lucas, the dynamo being their C40-1 model with a maximum output of 22 amps at 2 250 rev/min; the alternator is the 16ACR model with an output of 34 amps at 6 000 rev/min (equivalent to 2 800 engine rev/min). This type of alternator has a transistor-assisted voltage regulator located inside the alternator body; being of the self-excited type, no external field-isolating relay and charge-indicator unit are required.

On dynamo-equipped models, the voltage regulator is mounted under the bonnet on the bulkhead and does not normally need any attention. If any trouble occurs with the control box, the car will have to be returned to a British Leyland dealer so that checks can be made with a moving-coil voltmeter. Also under the bonnet is a fusebox covered by a plastic cap; as well as the working fuses there are two spares, so always ensure that as they are used, they are replaced.

Other electrical equipment includes the sealed-beam headlamps, mounted inside the front grille; sidelamp/flashers under the front bumpers; rear-lamp assemblies and number-plate lamp; horn and head-lamp flasher; plus of course the heater motor. The electrical ignition circuit is covered in Chapter 7.

One original feature of the electrical system on the Clubman and 1275GT is the use of a printed-circuit board in the facia to eliminate the need for all the many wires normally located there. To gain access to the printed circuit the facia has to be completely dismantled as it is located behind the instruments.

FUSES
The plastic cover on the fusebox is a 'push fit' and once it has been removed the fuses can be seen.

63. The fusebox and its cover are positioned on the right-hand side of the engine compartment
This carries two fuses clipped in position and two spares.

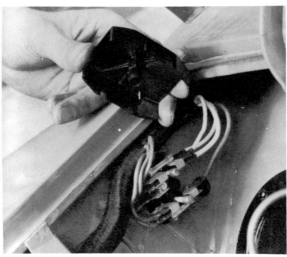

Across the A1–A2 terminals in the fusebox, the 35-amp 'blow-rated' fuse protects the auxiliary circuits which are independent of the ignition system, e.g. the horn and interior light. The other 35-amp 'blow-rated' fuse across terminals A3–A4, protects the auxiliary circuits, i.e. wiper motor, flasher indicators, heater motor, brake stoplamps, etc, which only operate when the ignition is switched on. The fuse rating quoted is the current that would cause the fuse to 'blow' in 10 seconds. At half the 'blowing' current, the fuse is capable of carrying the current continuously and it will not 'blow'.

A blown fuse is indicated by failure of all the units protected by it and can be confirmed simply by removing the fuse and examining it. The fuses clip in and out quite easily from the terminals and if a fuse has blown, the wire that can be seen running through the glass tube will be broken. Before simply replacing the fuse, however, it is always a wise precaution to check the wiring of the units covered by the fuse in case there is a fault which may have caused a short circuit. If there is such a fault it will cause the new fuse to blow also, so have it rectified before a further attempt is made to fit a new fuse.

There is also a 35-amp 'blow-rated' line fuse in the side and tail lighting circuit. It is situated in a cylindrical tube next to the wiring connectors on the engine bulkhead.

To renew this fuse, the cylinder must be gripped, its end pushed and twisted, and then pulled apart.

ROUTINE MAINTENANCE

The following routine attentions are required to the electrical system:

Topping up battery—Every week check the electrolyte level in the battery and, if necessary, top up with distilled water. Lift the covering on the boot floor and detach the cover that fits over the battery to expose the filler strip that runs along the top of the battery case. By looking into the holes, the level of the electrolyte can be seen; if the tops of the battery separator plates can be seen to be dry, add distilled water until it just covers the plates in each of the cells.

It is important that the battery is not overfilled, for on long journeys when the generator is charging at a high rate it is possible for the electrolyte to spill over, thereby covering everything in the vicinity with acid. In time this forms into a hard white substance and removes paint and ruins carpets and rubber mats, and the spare tyre if allowed to get that far.

Checking operation of equipment—At 5 000-km (3 000-mile) intervals, the lights, horn, indicators and windscreen wipers should be checked for correct functioning. If the owner gets into the habit of examining these items during this service it could well forestall a failure on the road. Any items found not to be working should be put right once the

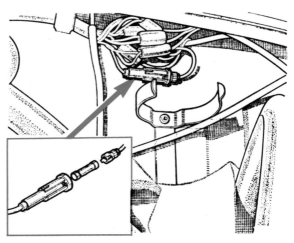

64. Line fuse for sidelamp and tail lamp circuit
The cylindrical tube containing the fuse is adjacent to the wiring connectors on the engine bulkhead.

source of the fault is ascertained; with the lights and indicators it is more-often-than-not bulb failures, but if the horn or wipers do not work they must be traced to determine whether it is the unit itself, the wiring or the switch.

65. Lubrication of dynamo (d.c. generator) rear bearing
The bronze-bush rear bearing of the dynamo is lubricated by adding two drops of engine oil through lubrication hole.
Avoid excessive lubrication to prevent possibility of oil reaching the commutator and dynamo brushes so affecting the charging rate of the dynamo.
The front ball bearing of the dynamo is pre-packed with grease and no lubrication is required.

Check the condition of the windscreen wiper blades—if they leave smear marks on the screen, or the rubber shows signs of perishing, then fit a new pair.

Check the headlamp beam alignment—this should be carried out by a British Leyland dealer as they have the correct Lucas beam setting equipment. Incorrectly aligned beams cause a definite traffic hazard at night so it is worth the small expense in having them set properly. As a temporary measure, however, they can be set by the owner as described later.

Dynamo rear-bearing lubrication—Every 10 000 km (6 000 miles), the dynamo end bush-bearing should be lubricated. At the rear of the dynamo a cylindrical extension carries the bush in which runs the commutator shaft, and in the end of the extension is a small hole. With an oilcan add one or two drops of oil to this hole, but no more. If the bearing is over-lubricated the oil will find its way onto the armature and impair its efficiency.

BATTERY

The battery fitted as original equipment is one of the following Lucas types: CL7 or CLZ7 with a capacity of 34 ampere-hours; CL9 or CLZ9 with a capacity of 40 Ah, but of course any battery-maker's corresponding model can be used as a replacement at a later date. The following instructions are to give the owner the necessary information to keep the unit in its best possible condition.

Checking the battery

The battery and its surrounding parts must be kept clean and dry, particularly the tops of the cells, as dampness can cause a slow short circuit between the securing strap and the positive terminal which will slowly run down the battery. Always clean off any corrosion from the battery bolts, straps and tray with diluted ammonia, afterwards painting the affected parts with anti-sulphuric paint.

At regular intervals inspect the terminal posts and, if they show signs of corrosion, remove the terminals and clean both terminals and posts in diluted ammonia. Smear them all with petroleum jelly before remaking the connections and make sure the securing screws are tight.

For those owners who have hydrometers, the specific gravity readings and their indications are given below:

Climates below 27°C (80°F)
Fully-charged   1·270 to 1·290
Half-charged   1·190 to 1·210
Discharged   1·110 to 1·130
Climates above 27°C (80°F)
Fully-charged   1·210 to 1·230
Half-charged   1·130 to 1·150
Discharged   1·050 tp 1·070

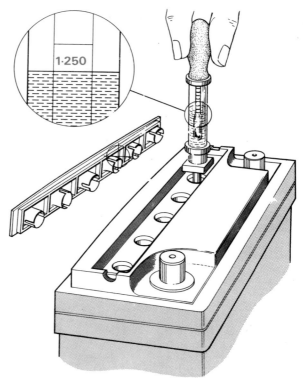

66. Using a hydrometer to ascertain the specific gravity of the electrolyte in the battery

The float reading obtained will indicate the state of charge of the battery as given in the accompanying table.
When taking a reading, the hydrometer float must be free—do not draw in too much electrolyte.

These figures are given assuming an electrolyte temperature of 16°C (60°F). If the temperature exceeds this, 0·002 must be added to the hydrometer reading for each 3°C (5°F) rise; similarly 0·002 must be subtracted for each drop of 3°C in temperature to give the correct specific gravity.

When a battery discharges in a short space of time it should be removed from the car for inspection. First, check the electrolyte levels and top up if necessary. Look carefully around the battery casing for cracks, which may be indicated by external corrosion or extreme variation in the hydrometer readings. If the casing *is* cracked, there is no alternative but to renew the unit.

Battery charging

It is not possible to say how long a battery must be left on a charger when recharging, as it depends upon the specific gravity before commencing and the

69

charging rate used. However, the charging must continue until all the cells are gassing freely at a rate of 3·5 amps and the specific gravity in all six cells has reached a maximum—i.e. no visible change over a period of four hours. At the end of charging, the hydrometer readings should be as those listed previously. An important point to watch when recharging a battery is that the temperature of the electrolyte must not be allowed to exceed 43°C (110°F) at any time. If this figure is ever reached, unclip the charger and suspend operations until the temperature falls at least 6°C (10°F). If this is not done, the life of the battery will be shortened.

Should the car be laid up for several weeks, perhaps over the winter months, it is advisable to remove the battery completely and store it in a warm, dry place. At regular periods check the level of the electrolyte and top it up if necessary, smear the terminal posts with petroleum jelly and keep the vent plug holes clear. Before replacing the battery prior to using the car again it must be recharged as described above.

DYNAMO

A Lucas C40-1 dynamo and a RB 106/2 control box are used and the charging circuit is wired through a bulb in the speedometer head so that any drop-off in charging when the engine is running can be immediately seen.

The voltage-control unit adjustment is sealed and it is important that this unit is not meddled with unless the owner is a skilled auto-electrician. This is because the voltage-control box ensures that under normal running conditions the battery receives a charge best suited to its state of storage. If the battery is in a discharged state, the control box allows the dynamo to give its full output. As the battery becomes

charged, the output from the dynamo is automatically reduced until, with a fully-charged battery, the dynamo gives only a trickle charge.

Removing the dynamo

As the drive-belt tension has been dealt with in Chapter 6, and lubrication of the dynamo rear bush bearing earlier in this chapter, it is now possible to proceed directly with the brush gear and commutator details. With these vehicles, the dynamo is of the type with no apertures in the outer casing through which access to the brush gear can be gained. Therefore, if any jobs need to be carried out on the unit it has to be removed completely from the engine. To do this, disconnect the wires from the dynamo terminals, marking them so they are replaced correctly, and remove the drive belt by slackening the dynamo pivot bolts as described in Chapter 6. Remove completely the two upper and one lower attachment bolts and the dynamo will come away and can be put on the bench.

Checking dynamo brush gear

The brushes are situated at the rear end of the dynamo (see Fig. 67) and to gain access to them the unit must be partly dismantled. Two long screw bolts hold the dynamo ends to the main casing, unscrew and withdraw these, whereupon the back-plate—complete with brush gear—can be removed.

There are three checks to make to the brush gear: (a) Test to see if they are sticking in their holders. If they are, lift them from the holders, clean them with a little petrol, and lightly ease the sides with a smooth file. Replace them in their original positions. (b) Test the brush-spring tension (the springs which bear down on the back of the brushes when they are in position). These should be between 510 and 737

67. Exploded view of Lucas C40-1 dynamo

1. Commutator end-bracket
2. Brush-tension spring
3. Oiler
4. Commutator
5. Armature shaft
6. Armature-shaft key
7. Shaft nut
8. Drive end-bracket
9. Through bolts
10. Lucar terminal for field current
11. Brush
12. Lucar terminal for generating current

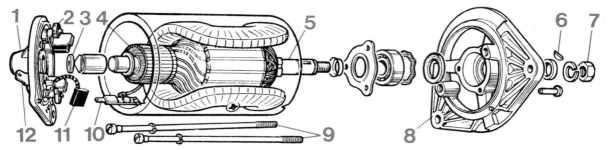

grammes (18 and 26 oz); if the tension is low fit new springs.

(c) If the brushes are worn down to 6 mm ($\frac{1}{4}$ in) or below, they must be renewed by undoing the small screw securing the brush wire to the holder and lifting out the brush.

Commutator maintenance

The only job the average owner can do on the commutator is clean it. If, upon inspection, the commutator is dirty it can be cleaned by wiping with a petrol-damped rag, and if this only part-cleans it use a strip of fine glass paper to polish and finish off the job. When using this latter method it is important that the glass paper is held stationary on the commutator while the complete armature is turned, it is then polished evenly.

If the commutator is pitted and shows signs of burned spots it must be skimmed on a lathe; this is best left to a British Leyland dealer as it is a job for a specialist.

DYNAMO FAULTS AND REMEDIES
Low or no charge

This is immediately apparent as the warning light in the speedometer head either glows at medium revs and only dies out at very high revs, or it never extinguishes at all. The first check is always the dynamo drive-belt tension, if this is slack or broken then the dynamo is not being driven at the correct speed, or not being driven at all. Adjust the tension if required as described in Chapter 6.

If the fault is still apparent after this check, then look at the wiring between the dynamo and the control box. The dynamo terminal D must be connected to the control box terminal D, and likewise the two terminals F must be inter-connected.

Should all the wiring be in order, remove the dynamo from the car and carry out the checks to the brush gear and commutator described earlier. Replace the dynamo afterwards and see if there is any improvement.

If the trouble is *still* present any further checks should be left to an authorised dealer as a moving-coil voltmeter is required to find the exact location of the trouble, and it is doubtful that any average car owner will have this piece of equipment.

Noisy dynamo

If there is a twittering squeak from the front of the engine, which increases in volume with the speed of the engine it is possibly a faulty dynamo bearing. Remove the drive belt and run the engine for a few minutes without it; should the noise then not be present the fault lies either with the dynamo or the water pump. Having diagnosed this far, replace the belt and run the engine again, this time listening very

closely to each of these units until the noise is traced.

If the fault *is* with the dynamo remove it from the car and dismantle the ends as described earlier. The bearing is situated behind a retaining plate in the front end-piece. It is easy to replace if Fig. 67 is consulted and the parts shown assembled as they are there. Do not forget to add a few drops of oil to the bush in the rear end of the unit.

ALTERNATOR

As mentioned at the beginning of this chapter, the Lucas 16ACR alternator (a.c. generator) may be fitted instead of the Lucas C40-1 dynamo (d.c. generator).

Alternator maintenance

The alternator does not require routine lubrication. Its shaft runs in two ball bearings which are pre-packed with grease for life.

The tension of its drive belt should be checked regularly in the same way as for a dynamo drive belt (see Chapter 6 under 'Fan belt'). An alternator belt is under greater stress than a dynamo belt so its condition may deteriorate faster.

Unlike dynamo brushes, alternator brushes do not handle the main output current of the machine. The two alternator brushes pass only a small direct current via two slip rings to and from the rotor field winding, which produces the rotating magnetic field. The brushes are housed in a moulding which is attached by screws to the alternator rear-end bracket under the moulded-terminal cover. The brushes bear on face-type slip-rings carried on the end-face of a small-diameter moulded drum attached to the rotor shaft, the inner slip-ring being centred on the shaft axis.

The brushes should be checked for condition at 120 000 km (75 000 miles). Access to the brushes is gained by detaching the moulded-terminal cover of the alternator, and undoing the two screws that secure each brush in its holder and which also connect each brush to a lead from the adjacent voltage regulator. The brushes and their coil springs can then be withdrawn from the holders. If a brush has worn down to a length of 9.5 mm ($\frac{3}{8}$ in), the complete brush set should be renewed.

Test that the brushes move freely in their holders. If not, the sides of the brushes should be cleaned with a petrol-moistened cloth. A leaf spring is located at the side of the centre brush; this must be refitted when the brushes are replaced.

Remove any oil, fluff and dust obstructing the flow of cooling air through the apertures of the slip-ring end-bracket and moulded terminal cover.

Precautions with alternator

To prevent damage to the alternator and its regu-

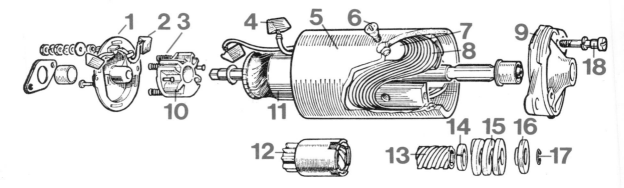

68. Exploded view of Lucas M35J starter motor

1. Commutator end-bracket
2. Bush housing
3. Brush springs
4. Brushes
5. Yoke
6. Pole screw
7. Pole shoe
8. Field coils
9. Drive end-bracket
10. Brush box mouldings
11. Armature
12. Pinion and barrel
13. Screwed sleeve
14. Buffer washer
15. Main spring
16. Spring cup
17. Circlip
18. Drive end-bracket bolt

lator, the following precautions must be observed:

When fitting a battery, make absolutely certain which are the battery's positive (+) and negative (−) terminals and be sure to connect its negative terminal to earth.

Do not disconnect the battery or any lead in the charging circuit without first switching off the ignition. If any lead in the charging circuit, including the battery, is disconnected during servicing, ensure that all leads are properly connected before running the engine.

If for any reason the engine has to be run with the charging circuit incomplete, remove all socket connections from the alternator terminals.

STARTER

The Lucas type M35J starter motor used on all models is situated on the engine flywheel housing, the side of the engine that faces the front of the car, low down beneath the distributor. The starter-motor switch is combined with the ignition switch, so that the key is turned a quarter-turn to open the ignition circuit, then turned further against a spring return to operate the starter motor. The starter switch works through a solenoid that is mounted on top of the flywheel housing and from this the main heavy duty cable runs back to the battery and down to the starter.

The starter is of the usual pinion drive type, where the pinion is carried on a barrel assembly running on a screwed sleeve. When the starter switch is operated, the armature and the screwed sleeve (which is on

the end of the armature shaft) commence to rotate. The barrel assembly does not rotate at once, but lags slightly behind the armature, with the result that it moves along the screwed sleeve and engages with the flywheel ring gear. A shock-absorber spring is situated in the pinion barrel and this takes the impact of the engagement. With the pinion mating to the flywheel gear, the starter will turn the engine. As soon as the engine fires and commences to run, the flywheel is driven faster by the engine than the starter motor. The barrel therefore overruns the armature shaft and is screwed back along its sleeve, thereby coming out of mesh with the flywheel gear.

Testing the starter

If the starter refuses to turn the engine when the switch is operated, the first check should always be the battery. If the battery is known to be in tip-top condition, the following checks should be made:

Switch on the lamps and operate the starter motor. If the lights go dim, but the starter is not heard to turn, then it is an indication that the current is flowing through the starter windings but the pinion is meshed with the flywheel gear and stuck there. Where this happens, the pinion can be freed from the flywheel ring gear with a spanner applied to the squared end of the armature shaft; do not use excessive leverage or the shaft could be bent.

If the lamps do not go dim when the starter switch is operated, check that the solenoid switch is working properly. Move from this to the battery connections, switch connections and starter connections. Remove and clean terminals if necessary and check the condition of the wiring between these units—fitting new pieces of cable where needed.

Sluggish or slow action of the starter is usually caused by poor connections which make a high resistance in the circuit. Make the checks to the wiring described above. If the starter pinion is heard to come into mesh with the flywheel, but the engine does not turn, then damaged teeth on the pinion or flywheel gear are indicated.

Checking brushes and commutator

Remove the starter motor from the engine by disconnecting the cables from their terminals on the end of the motor and taking out the bolts that pass through the starter flange and into the flywheel housing. It is always a good idea to disconnect the battery earth terminal before tampering with any part of the electrical system, to avoid a short circuit. Withdraw the starter and place it on a work bench.

This particular starter is fitted with a face-type commutator and has no apertures through the outer casing to gain access to the brushes. Take out the two setscrews that secure the commutator end-bracket, detach the bracket from the yoke, disengage the field brushes from the brush gear and remove the bracket.

Brushes should be renewed if they are found to be approaching their minimum allowed length of 9·5 mm (0·375 in). A soldering iron will be needed to disconnect the brush wires from their connection points and the new brushes soldered in exactly the same place.

The brush springs that fit into the brush holder should have their tensions checked by fitting the brushes into their respective positions and then using a push-type spring gauge on each brush in turn until the brush protrudes approximately 1·5 mm (0·062 in) from the holder. When this point is reached, the gauge should be reading approximately 794 gm (28 oz). If it is found that one or more of the brush springs has lost its tension it will mean a completely new commutator end-bracket has to be purchased as the springs cannot be renewed singularly.

It is possible to have the commutator re-surfaced on a lathe when it shows signs of pitting or wear, but it is more practical to obtain and fit a Lucas factory exchange unit. Unless the owner has some experience with dismantling electrical units he is probably wiser to let a dealer take care of any faults within the starter motor.

LIGHTING SYSTEM

The headlamps are Lucas sealed-beam units with no separate bulbs and the fixing and adjusting screws are covered on each side by moulded extension

pieces of the radiator grille. Sidelamps and flasher lamps are situated under the front bumper at each side, whilst the rear/stop lamps and rear flashers are in a combined assembly that slightly wraps-around each rear corner of the car.

LAMP UNITS AND BULBS

The wattage of the 12-volt bulbs are as follows:

	Wattage
Sealed-beam headlamps	45/60
Sidelamps and flasher repeaters	6
Flasher direction indicators	21
Number-plate lamps	6
Tail/stoplamps	6/21
Interior lamp	6
Panel and Warning lamps	2·2

Renewing sealed-beam headlamps

The headlamp cover can be removed by taking out the four Phillips (cross-head) self-tapping screws, whereupon it will expose the screws that secure the headlamp unit to the body. The two cheese-headed screws at the top and side are for beam alignment and it is the three cross-head screws (2), Fig. 69, that should be taken out to free the unit.

Withdraw the headlamp unit and tilt it forward so

69. Headlamp removal

First take off the extension panel (1), secured by four cross-head screws, then remove the three cross-head screws (2) securing the inner rim. With the inner rim removed, the light unit will come away from its housing and thus allow the three-pin plug carrying the wiring to be disconnected from its holder.

Screws (3) and (4) are for adjusting the alignment of the beam.

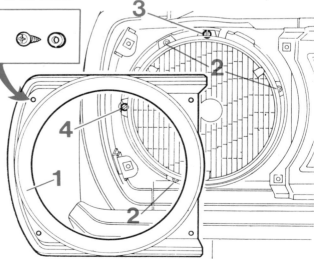

that the plug-in connector can be seen; detach the plug and the unit is free. There is no bulb as such, the electrical filament being encased directly in the glass and reflector. A complete new sealed-beam unit is needed when the headlamp fails and these can be obtained from any British Leyland dealer. Offer up the new unit and replace the connector plug, then secure it with the three screws.

After a new headlamp unit has been fitted it is generally necessary to have the beams reset to ensure that other drivers are not being dazzled. This is covered later in the chapter.

Finally, refit the front-grille extension cover over the headlamp and tighten the four cross-head screws.

Sidelamps and flashers

Two screws secure the amber and clear lens over each light fitting beneath the front bumper. When the screws are out, the lens will come away and expose the bulbs behind. These bulbs are both of the bayonet-type fitting and to remove have to be pressed into their holders and turned to release the bayonet pins, then withdrawn. The new bulb can be inserted exactly opposite to this.

70. Printed circuit at back of facia panel— Clubman models illustrated
Each of the square holes in the printed circuit is an aperture for a facia panel bulb.
1. *Printed circuit*
2. *Printed-circuit securing stud*
3. *Fuel and temperature gauge securing screws*
4. *Panel and warning lamp bulb holders*
5. *Voltage stabiliser*

When replacing the lens, do not overtighten the screws as the plastic that the lens is made from may crack around the holes.

Stop/tail lamps and flashers

The same principle applies as with the sidelamps in that the plastic red/amber lens is secured to a chrome surround by means of two screws. Take out the screws and the lens will come away, exposing the bulbs.

The stop/tail bulb is a twin-filament type and to ensure that it is not fitted the wrong way round, the bayonet pins are offset. When removing the bulb by pressing in and turning, note which side the high pin and which side the low pin is located, then offer up the new bulb in the same way.

Flasher bulbs are of the normal single-filament type that can be fitted any way round, the bayonet pins being in the same position on each side of the bulb cap.

Number-plate lamps

Access to the two festoon-type bulbs on saloon cars is gained by removing the lens securing screws and then easing the lens and bulb holder from the lamp.

On the Clubman Estate there are two lamps positioned at each side of the number plate. Access to one of the bayonet-fixing bulbs is gained after removing the domed cover and glass (single screw).

Panel lamps

As the facia instruments all work through a printed circuit board, the complete nacelle with all instruments installed can be quite easily removed. Take

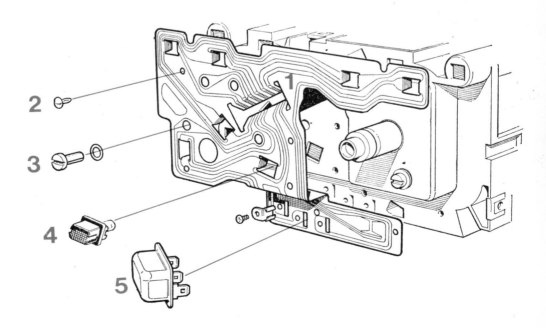

out the small screws at top and bottom of each side of the instrument nacelle and pull the complete assembly forward until the connections at the back are exposed. With the Clubman there is only the speedometer cable and the multi-plug wiring connector to the printed circuit; the speedometer cable can be disconnected by lifting the little release lever so that the cable detaches from the back of the instrument; the multi-plug connector pulls straight out of the back of the printed-circuit board.

Additionally with the 1275GT there are two wire connections to the back of the tachometer and its own illuminating bulb holder.

With the connections detached, tilt the complete instrument assembly forward so that the back (printed circuit) can be seen. Across the top can be seen four bulb holders that are simple snap-fits into the printed circuit, there are three more near the lower edge of the printed circuit. Withdraw whichever bulb holder contains the faulty bulb, fit a new bulb and snap the holder back into the printed circuit.

Remake all the connections at the back of the instrument nacelle and screw the assembly back into place on the facia.

HEADLAMP BEAMSETTING
Reference has been made to the importance of correct beamsetting already in this chapter, this being due to the road safety factor involved. Headlamps should be set so that when they are on high beam, the beams are parallel with the road surface. If adjustment is required then the lamp covers (front grille extensions) must be removed as described under 'Renewing sealed-beam headlamps', so that the adjusting screws can be reached.

Set the car on a level surface about 2·70 m (9 ft) from a plain vertical wall and switch on the headlamps in the high-beam position. The beam pattern will be seen on the wall, the centres of which should be at the same height and distance apart as the centres of the corresponding headlamps. Use the top adjusting screw (3), Fig. 69, on each headlamp unit to raise or lower the beam, and the side screw (4) to set the beam pointing straight ahead.

Although the method of setting the beams described here is satisfactory as a temporary measure (such as after fitting a new headlamp unit) it is preferable to have them accurately set by a British Leyland dealer on a Lucas beamsetter. This should be carried out every 5 000 km (3 000 miles) as it is possible for the headlamp units to get out of adjustment.

WINDSCREEN WIPERS
A Lucas wiper motor is fitted, the model being Type 14W which is available either in single, or two-speed form. If windscreen wiper failure occurs always

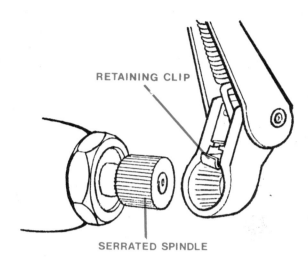

RETAINING CLIP

SERRATED SPINDLE

71. Windscreen wiper-arm adjustment
The arm can be repositioned on the serrated spindle after raising retaining clip.

check the fuse first. If this is in order, the problem could be a faulty switch, or the motor itself.

As far as normal maintenance is concerned, the only action required is occasional (every 12 months at least) changing of the wiper blades. To remove these from their arms is quite easy; lift the arm away from the windscreen against the tension of its spring and holding it in this position, slide the wiper blade off the curved end.

If the spring tension goes on the wiper arm a new one should be fitted, otherwise the wipers will tend to lift from the screen when travelling at speed. Lift the wiper arm away from the screen and a spring clip will be seen where the arm fits over the drive splines. Prise the spring clip up with a small screwdriver and pull the arm off its splines. Fit the new arm in the same position on the splines, or it might 'smack' against the lower edge of the windscreen when the wipers are running.

FLASHER UNIT
The Lucas two-terminal flasher unit is located behind an aperture in the facia parcel shelf, being held in position by a spring clip holder.

Should one of the flasher bulbs fail, warning of this is given by: (1) the indicator warning light on the facia staying on all the time (not flashing on/off); (2) by lack of ticking noise normally associated with the flashers working, and (3) the other flasher bulb on the same side of the car remaining on and not flashing when the signal stalk is operated for that side of the car.

When this happens, a new bulb should be fitted as soon as possible so that the flasher system is operational again in the shortest possible time.

If none of the flashers work, the first check is always with the flasher unit itself (providing the A3–A4 fuse has been ruled out). Pull the flasher unit from its clip and withdraw it through the aperture in the parcel shelf. Have the new flasher unit ready and simply pull off the wiring to the terminals and fit them to the respective terminals on the new unit. This can then be reinserted in its spring clip holder.

If the flashers still do not work after checking bulbs, fuses, and flasher unit, then the fault could lie with the stalk switch on the steering column, or the wiring. In either case it is best left to a dealer to make the necessary checks.

KEY TO COMPONENTS FOR WIRING DIAGRAMS

1. Dynamo
2. Control box
3. 12-volt battery
4. Starter solenoid
5. Starter motor
6. Lighting switch
7. Headlamp dip switch
8. R.H. headlamp
9. L.H. headlamp
10. Main-beam warning lamp
11. R.H. sidelamp
12. L.H. sidelamp
14. Panel lamps
15. Number-plate lamp(s)
16. R.H. stop and tail lamp
17. L.H. stop and tail lamp
18. Stoplamp switch
19. Fuseblock
20. Interior light
21. R.H. door switch
22. L.H. door switch
23. Horn(s)
24. Hornpush
25. Flasher unit
26. Combined direction indicator/headlamp flasher/headlamp high-low beam
27. Direction-indicator warning lamp
28. R.H. front-flasher lamp
29. L.H. front-flasher lamp
30. R.H. rear-flasher lamp
31. L.H. rear-flasher lamp
32. Heater or fresh-air blower switch (where fitted)
33. Heater or fresh-air blower motor (where fitted)
34. Fuel gauge
35. Fuel-gauge tank unit
36. Windscreen-wiper switch
37. Windscreen-wiper motor
38. Ignition/starter switch
39. Ignition coil
40. Distributor
42. Oil-pressure switch
43. Oil-pressure warning lamp
44. Ignition warning lamp
45. Speedometer
46. Coolant-temperature gauge
47. Coolant-temperature transmitter
64. Bi-metal instrument voltage stabiliser
67. Line fuse (35-amp 'blow' rated)
75. Automatic-transmission safety switch (where fitted)
77. Electric windscreen washer
78. Electric windscreen-washer switch
83. Induction heater and thermostat (where fitted)
84. Suction-chamber heater (where fitted)
95. Tachometer (1275GT)
110. R.H. repeater flasher (where fitted)
111. L.H. repeater flasher (where fitted)
115. Rear-window demister switch (where fitted)
116. Rear-window demister unit (where fitted)
139. Alternative connections for two-speed wiper motor and switch (where fitted)
150. Rear-window demister warning light (where fitted)
152. Hazard warning light (where fitted)
153. Hazard warning switch (where fitted)
154. Hazard warning flasher unit
158. Printed-circuit instrument panel

CABLE COLOUR CODE FOR WIRING DIAGRAMS

B. Black	G. Green	W. White
U. Blue	P. Purple	Y. Yellow
N. Brown	R. Red	LG. Light Green

When a cable has two colour code letters, the first denotes the main colour and the second denotes the tracer colour.

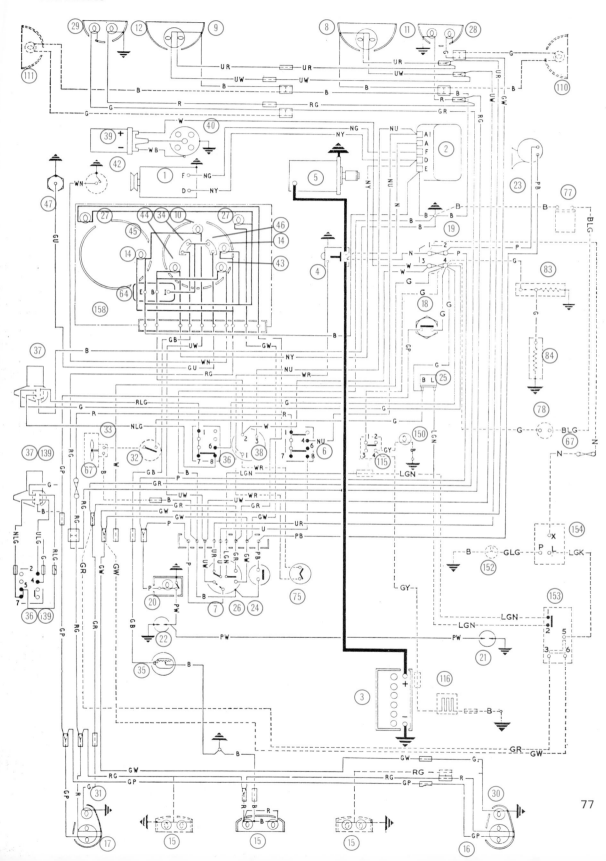

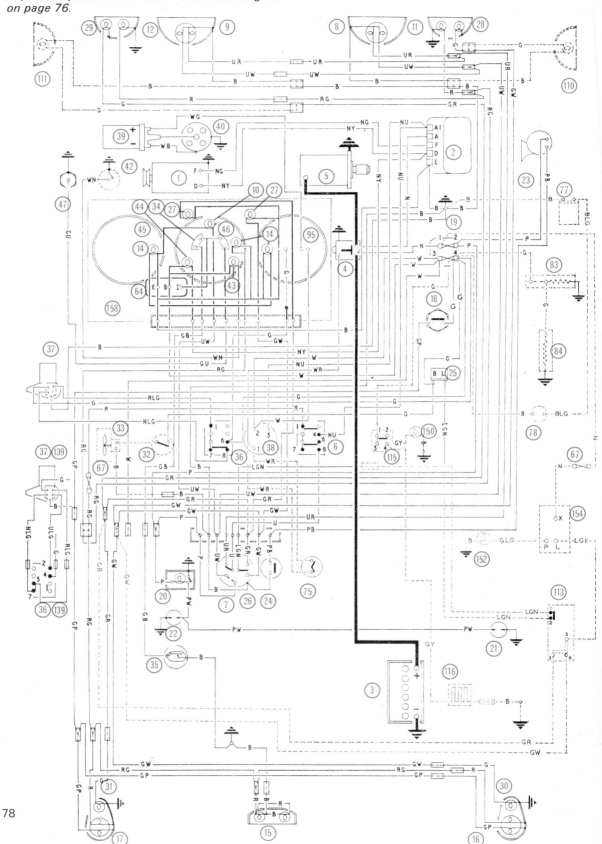

Index

© The Hamlyn Publishing Group Limited 1974
First Edition 1974
Published by the Hamlyn Publishing Group Limited
London · New York · Sydney · Toronto
Astronaut House, Feltham, Middlesex, England

ISBN 0 600 36083 0

Origination and Phototypesetting by V Siviter Smith Limited,
Birmingham
Printed and Bound in Great Britain by Fleetway Printers Limited,
Gravesend, Kent.